Advertising and Identity in Europe

The I of the Beholder

Edited by
Jackie Cannon
Patricia Anne Odber de Baubeta
Robin Warner

intellect™
Bristol, UK
Portland, OR, USA

First Published in Great Britain in Hardback in 2000 by
Intellect Books, PO Box 862, Bristol BS99 1DE, UK

First Published in USA in 2000 by
Intellect Books, ISBS, 5824 N.E. Hassalo St, Portland, Oregon 97213-3644, USA

Consulting Editor: Robin Beecroft
Copy Editor: Jeremy Lockyer

A catalogue record for this book is available from the British Library

ISBN 1-84150-037-2

Printed and bound in Great Britain by Cromwell Press, Wiltshire

Contents

Acknowledgements

The editors wish to express their most sincere thanks to all the representatives of the various institutions which have made a significant contribution to both the original conference event in May 1999 and the subsequent publication of this volume. Special thanks go to Professor Trevor Dadson of the Department of Hispanic Studies at the University of Birmingham who supported the hosting of the one-day conference as well as this publication; Professor Seán Hand of the School of Languages at Oxford Brookes University and Professor Nicholas Round of the Department of Hispanic Studies at the University of Sheffield as well as to Professor Michael Scriven of the Faculty of Languages and European Studies at the University of the West of England. We are greatly indebted also to Salvador Estébanez at the Instituto Cervantes in Manchester who embraced the opportunity to invite Professor J. Enrique Bigné from the Marketing Department at the Universitat Jaume I to speak at the conference, thus allowing us to enhance the inter-disciplinary nature of the event. Further thanks are extended to the Association for Contemporary Iberian Studies which, through regular conference events, has long encouraged the exchange of ideas and has provided a forum for common interests to be explored.

We thank also colleagues, the essays of a number of whom are included in this volume, who confirmed the importance of this area of study by either offering papers at or attending the conference and who subsequently encouraged us to proceed with this publication. Those whose contributions are included are further thanked for the conscientiousness with which they have collaborated with the editors in submitting, reviewing, revising and finalising their papers within the required time-scale.

Many other people have also played a substantial part in allowing the editors to move forward with this volume. Amongst those who deserve special thanks are Hilary Rollin, John Jepson and D.W. Baubeta.

Preface

This volume of essays had its genesis in an international symposium held at the University of Birmingham in May 1999. While the organisers were well aware that advertising and identity were topic areas which were each in their own right well-established, the opportunity to explore the interface was to produce an overwhelming response in terms of papers offered, audience attendance and participation, and subsequent feedback and requests for further information. The symposium attracted contributions from a wide range of countries, languages and disciplines. The latter included Applied Language Studies, Cultural Studies, Gender Studies, Marketing, Media Studies and Translation Studies. Participants came from Denmark, England, France, the Irish Republic, Portugal, Scotland and Spain. Texts under scrutiny were variously in Catalan, English, French, German, Portuguese and Spanish.

The present volume is not the published proceedings of the conference. Rather, it represents in all cases a process of reflection on and further development of ideas originally presented in that forum. The explicit speculation that is characteristic of conferences has been transformed into a more thorough exploration, documentation and application of scholarly apparatus. Having initially tested their ideas, many of the contributors have benefited from the response of colleagues as an aid to reflection, revision and consolidation. As a result of this evolutionary process, the narrow thematic groupings of the conference have been revised and refocused.

Our definition of advertising is not restricted to texts intended to sell products and services, but is understood to include promotional texts of all kinds whose function is to inform and persuade. Whatever we think about advertising, it has to be recognised that it is a pervasive part of daily life; we are surrounded by advertising texts demanding our attention. In addition, we encounter a variety of texts which, at first sight, appear to be of another type, but in fact fulfil many of the functions, overt and covert, of advertising.

Advertisers have long been aware of the need to target specific groups of consumers and to appeal to them precisely in terms of their sense of membership of such groups. Our post-industrial society is characterised by greatly altered work and leisure patterns as well as a weakening of national and communal frameworks for collective identity. The interrelated questions 'Who am I? Who are we?' are becoming increasingly difficult to answer. We would maintain that theories relating to identity have thus become central to current advertising practice, which not only reflects but actively makes use of such concerns. The papers in this volume explore the different constructions of regional, national, social and sexual identities exploited by advertisers to render their messages effective.

The fourteen contributions collected here share the underlying premise that advertising is inherently and necessarily enmeshed in the broad cultural experience of those at whom it is aimed. The issues they address range from the marketing effectiveness of identity factors and consumers' changing awareness of such elements to the role of advertising in shaping as well as reflecting these changes and its contribution to perceptions of social, professional and gender roles. The validity of advertisements as cultural artefacts and the contribution to processes of signification of visual and verbal interplay are also considered.

The papers have been grouped in thematic clusters, although, in accordance with the inter-disciplinary nature of the initial conference, inevitably there will be overlap. A number of the contributors bring a neutral analytical perspective to the aspects they analyse, examining broad trends and incidences of noteworthy features, assessing the efficacy of different options or highlighting the creative and stylistic qualities of the promotional texts. Others adopt in principle a critical stance towards the function of advertising, either in itself or as an important component of cultural mediation in general, drawing attention to the way promotional discourse inevitably favours certain positions in the ideological contests characteristic of the postmodern age.

The first cluster of papers centres on the perception of consumer identity in the advertising practices of various European countries, both in terms of the target sectors and the companies and advertisers issuing the adverts. Bigné reflects upon attitudes in other European countries to Spanish manufactured goods and agricultural produce, concluding that the country of origin as a marketing element has a positive impact on consumer perceptions in the case of certain product sectors. What is apparent is that while agricultural products enjoy relatively high prestige, manufactured goods from Spain suffer compared with, say, German products. Cannon, on the other hand, argues that the lack of prestige associated with Spain as the country of origin is largely due to a reluctance on the part of Spanish manufacturers and advertisers to make use of features of national identity. This unwillingness, stemming at least partly from Spain's political past, has resulted in a conscious determination to become European while at the same time strengthening the image of the autonomous regions. By contrast, the German industrial sector has been able to adopt perceptions of excellence and expertise in engineering as uncontestable national qualities. Indeed, Head asserts that, instead of standardising advertising practices and eradicating the need to foreground national differences, globalisation allows manufacturers and advertisers to make use of these positive perceptions which are built upon commonly accepted national stereotypes.

One of the most obvious ways in which promotional texts make use of concepts of identity is in the area which can be broadly denoted by the various senses of the term 'address'. This issue is considered in the second cluster. In a more strictly linguistic application, McLaren deals with pronouns which realise direct and indirect address as part of her contrastive survey of writer self-reference and persuasive techniques in French and English promotional brochures. Damamme-Gilbert also analyses French advertisements, although she draws on a broader European theoretical tradition concerned with the way messages are designed to address receivers by constructing for them an interactive and socially conditioned position – an identity. The second two papers in this group also comment upon techniques of persuasion. Crompton & McAlea start from the observation that the producers of advertisements are fully aware of the devices – if not the traditional names for them – employed for purposes of persuasion in classical times. Through a close analysis of two television advertisements in English and Spanish, they demonstrate the range and complexity of the rhetorical strategies deployed in these relatively brief and apparently guileless items. Warner compares the ways in which coherence is sustained for individuals' sense of self-identity with the contribution of argumentation to discourse coherence, arguing that advertisers exploit the affinity between these two processes. It is precisely by making coherent choices among lifestyle options – in effect making sense of their lives – that addressees are expected to make sense of advertisers' persuasive claims.

Our third cluster deals with Catalonia and Portugal and their respective languages and identities. One option available to advertisers concerns the choice of language in which they advertise. The issue of language is of fundamental importance in Spain where four languages officially coexist. Buffery examines a little-researched aspect of the language of advertising, the advertising of language through politically motivated campaigns conducted in Catalan to promote the language itself and, by extension, a collective regional identity. By contrast, Portuguese national identity, while difficult to define, is so firmly established that it becomes yet another refrain in the advertisers' repertoire. Odber presents a study of advertisements which deliberately make use of historical Portuguese achievements and related icons to promote the widest possible range of products and services. Continuing this scrutiny of Portuguese national pride, Oliveira studies the reactions in the quality and tabloid press to Portugal's first winner of the Nobel Prize for Literature, with a detailed critical focus on the appropriation of individual achievement for the purpose of enhancing national self-image. In the light of her examination of a specific Portuguese product sector, Água-Mel concludes that wine advertising in the domestic market perpetuates traditional stereotypes of acceptable male and female behaviour, regardless of whether these truly reflect the gender roles of post-revolutionary Portuguese society.

The final cluster looks mainly at televisual advertising as an expression of popular culture. The neo-Gramscian view of popular culture as a key arena in the transitional struggle between neo-liberalism and persistent forms associated with earlier socio-political models allows O'Donnell to assess the importance of postmodern trends in television advertising. The relative paucity of postmodern motifs in ads framed by soap operas, and especially in Southern as opposed to Northern Europe, may be ascribed to factors such as the target audience and transnational economic practice. From a similar perspective, Moody argues that the plethora of nostalgic texts and motifs used in print and television advertising for tea in Britain was calculated to soften the impact of the constraints imposed by successive governments as a response to the new world economic order from the 1970s onwards. Through her analysis, she demonstrates how heritage and patriotic values are manipulated in order to palliate the social and political reality. White also focuses on popular culture and nostalgia, comparing and contrasting television advertising in both France and Britain during the World Cup in 1998. Particular attention is given to the roles performed by players, commentators and spectators in the intersecting domains of football and advertising, highlighting a mismatch between traditional perceptions of masculinity and new, ambivalent representations of male identity.

What emerges from this collection of essays is the manifest need for further research into an area which provides an opportunity for genuinely interdisciplinary study. By investigating the complex interrelationship between forms of advertising and constructs of identity, we are afforded a greater understanding of both.

1   Image and Spanish Country of Origin Effect

J. Enrique Bigné
Universitat Jaume I, Spain

Introduction

The aim of this paper is to analyse the 'made in' or country of origin effect. The first studies on the subject appeared in the 1970s and since then a lot of research papers have discussed both the existence and argued relevance of the country of origin as an identifiable selling feature. Peterson & Jolibert (1995) counted more than two hundred papers on the topic published in international journals and presented at conferences. This current study is based on the preliminary idea that the country of origin of a product is an extrinsic attribute that influences consumer assessment of that product.

Some argue that the country of origin has little impact on product selection while others believe that this additional attribute allows clearer differentiation between products (Bilkey & Nes, 1982; Papadopoulos & Heslop, 1993; Peterson & Jolibert, 1995). Nevertheless, there are certain features which influence the impact of the country of origin effect. These include increased trade flows; greater standardisation of products; closer economic integration exemplified by the European Union and Mercosur in South America; and more common international division of production, resulting in hybrid products (Ettenson & Gaeth, 1991). A new phenomenon has emerged: products are made in more than one country. This is the case of a personal computer whose parts are made in Taiwan, Indonesia, Malaysia or wherever, assembled in Germany, and sold, perhaps, in South America. These patterns work in favour of the importance of country of origin effect. In fact, the country of origin may be seen as a competitive advantage. In addition, some companies are now also using regional brands, like 'Made in Europe'. This new general brand is critical for the country of origin effect.

Conceptual framework

A general conceptual framework of country of origin can be seen in Figure 1. Three different effects can be distinguished: cognitive, affective and normative. They can have an influence on attitudes and preferences, both generic and for specific product categories made in one country. These are moderated by demographic and psychographic factors, such as personality, values and lifestyle and can affect consumers' buying intentions. Attitudes towards products made in one country involve an affective response involving positive or negative values, feelings or emotions triggered by the country or its products. Preference, on the other hand, reflects a choice between a number of options.

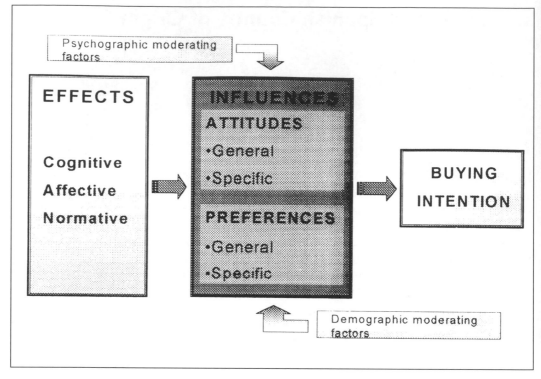

Figure 1. Conceptual framework of the country of origin

Our review of the literature has shown a lot of empirical research on this subject. Much of it has focused on testing the influence of the country of origin effect on attitudes, at the level of brands (D'Asthous & Ahmed, 1993; Eroglu & Machleit, 1989; Wall, Liefeld & Heslop, 1991), product categories (Cicic, Tsai & Patterson, 1993; Cordell, 1992; Minor & Hodges, 1993; Miquel, Newman, Bigné & Chansarkar, 1993), industrial products (Cattin, Jolibert & Lohnes, 1982; Kaynak & Cavusgil, 1983; Kaynak & Kucukemiroglu, 1992; White & Cundiff, 1978), consumer products (Babb, Lascu & Vann, 1993; Bannister & Saunders, 1978) and even the influence of the retailer (Chao, 1989; Han & Terpstra, 1988). On the other hand, some research has focused on the influence of country of origin effect on preferences, both generic (Chao, 1989; Etzel & Walker, 1974; Kaynak & Cavusgil, 1983) and for specific industrial products (Cattin, Jolibert & Lohnes, 1982; Nagashima, 1977).

As well as empirical research, some efforts have been made to develop conceptual frameworks that explain the country of origin/made in effect construct. It is necessary to evaluate the importance of each of the three aspects: cognitive, affective and normative.

There are two approaches to the cognitive aspect: one is known as the halo approach (Ericksson, Johansson & Chao, 1984; Johansson, Douglas & Nonaka, 1985) and the other one is the summary (Han, 1989). Country of origin as a halo directly

1   American people should always buy American-made products instead of imports.

2   Only those products that are unavailable in the US should be imported.

3   Buy American-made products. Keep America working.

4   American products first, last, and foremost.

5   Purchasing foreign-made products is un-American.

6   It is not right to purchase foreign products, because it puts Americans out of jobs.

7   A real American should always buy American-made products.

8   We should purchase products manufactured in America instead of letting other countries get rich off us.

9   It is always best to purchase American products

10 There should be very little trading or purchasing of goods from other countries unless out of necessity.

11 Americans should not buy foreign products, because this hurts American business and causes unemployment.

12 Curbs should be put on all imports.

13 It may cost me in the long-run but I prefer to support American products.

14 Foreigners should not be allowed to put their products on our markets.

15 Foreign products should be taxed heavily to reduce their entry into the US.

16 We should buy from foreign countries only those products that we cannot obtain within our own country.

17 American consumers who purchase products made in other countries are responsible for putting their fellow Americans out of work.

Source: Shimp & Sharma (1987)

Figure 2. CETSCALE.

affects consumers' beliefs about product attributes and indirectly affects overall evaluation of products through those beliefs:

country image ⇄beliefs ⇄brand attitude

and summary construct suggests the following relationships:

beliefs ⇄country image ⇄brand attitude.

For the affective aspect, two variables have been considered: beliefs (Ericksson, Johansson & Chao, 1984; Cordell, 1992) and attitudes (Han, 1989).

Finally a normative aspect, understood as the external and internal pressures on the consumer (Sharma, Shimp & Shin, 1995), has been more recently incorporated. This includes measuring ethnocentrism and the CETSCALE (Shimp & Sharma, 1987) which will be explained later.

The concept of ethnocentrism was originally developed in sociology almost a hundred years ago. Later, it was adapted to analysing consumer behaviour. As Shimp & Sharma (1987) pointed out, we can consider country of origin as a feature which influences beliefs held by consumers on the appropriateness, even the morality, of buying products made abroad. Shimp & Sharma (1987) measured this belief through a scale developed by them, known as the CETSCALE (Consumer Ethnocentrism Scale), plotting the responses to seventeen statements on a seven-point Likert scale. Figure 2 shows the scale proposed originally by Shimp & Sharma (1987).

Since then, only a few studies have been carried out using this scale in different cultures. Among them Netemeyer, Durvasula & Lichtenstein (1991) used it in Japan, the United States, Germany and France; Pecotich, Presley & Roth (1993) in Australia; and later Sharma, Shimp & Shin (1995) in Korea. No research has yet been carried out in a homogeneous cultural and socio-economic context such as the European Union. Sharma, Shimp & Shin (1995) also identified some moderating variables: some demographic and economic, such as gender, age, education and income, and some psychographic, like patriotism, cultural openness and perception of economic threat.

Objectives

Little research has been done on country of origin and consumer ethnocentrism at European level and even less in Spain. It was with this in mind that we carried out an empirical study in continuance of an earlier one, from 1991. Our current objectives are as follows.

Firstly, we want to study attitudes towards foreign products, and for some specific product categories made in Spain. As we discussed earlier, attitudes towards 'made in' as a product attribute are critical for later consumption.

Secondly, we aim to measure general and specific preferences towards product categories made in particular countries.

Thirdly, the appropriateness of buying products made abroad measured by the CETSCALE was investigated. This will lead to some explanations of consumers'

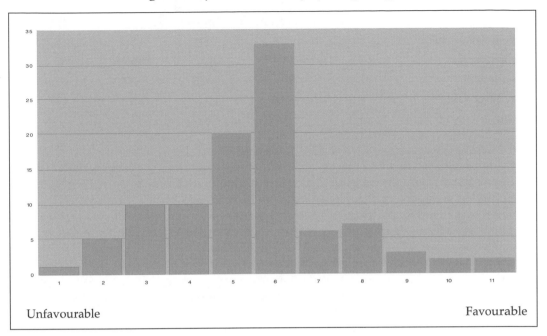

Graph 1. Bar diagram of feelings about buying foreign products (percentages).

behaviour regarding the choice of foreign versus national products. For these purposes, we carried out an empirical study in four European countries: France, Germany, Spain and the UK. We selected five product categories of great impact on the Spanish economy: footwear, toys, tourist resorts, oranges and wine, widely recognised by consumers in each country.

We used a personal interview to obtain information using the CETSCALE about individuals' degree of openness to foreign issues, the degree of knowledge of other countries, the degree of familiarity with the products, scales of specific attitudes to product categories, specific preference for product categories and ethnocentrism beliefs. We obtained a sample of 176 German respondents, 450 Spaniards, 173 from France and 206 from the UK.

Analysis of results

A survey carried out by Gallup gave us some preliminary information: 20,000 respondents from 20 different countries participated in the Gallup survey (Bozell-Gallup, 1994). In the worldwide survey, the most preferred countries were Japan, Germany, United States, United Kingdom and France. Within Europe: Germany, Japan, the United States, the UK and France were the most preferred countries.

In 1991, we undertook a study in Spain and the UK (Miquel, Bigné & Newman, 1993) from which we can conclude that:

- Spaniards preferred national products.
- The British view of Spanish products was neutral.

Attitude	France	Germany	Spain	UK	Total
Very unfavourable	3.6	3.6	6.0	5.7	5.1
Unfavourable	60.0	33.1	27.1	59.0	40.1
Favourable	32.1	55.4	56.0	33.1	47.5
Very favourable	4.2	7.8	10.5	2.1	7.3
Mean	5.2	5.8	5.86	5.1	5.6

Table 1. Feelings about buying foreign products (% vertical)

- Spanish fruit and vegetables had a clearly differentiated image.
- Spain has a low competitive position in wines, cars and toys.
- There was a low knowledge of Spanish brands.
- The best attributes for Spanish products were price, design and appearance.

Generic attitude towards foreign products

In order to analyse the general attitude towards foreign products, a question was asked regarding feelings about buying products manufactured abroad. The response was scored from 1 (very unfavourable) to 11 (very favourable).

Graph 1 shows the distribution of frequencies for the whole sample. Distribution is normal, with higher peaking in average values.

Table 1 shows the distribution of frequencies. We have divided feelings into four quartiles. From the table we can deduce that the respondents who express the most negative feelings are the French and the British, the least negative feelings towards foreign products being expressed by Germans and Spaniards. The mean values also show the situation of each group of respondents.

The variance analysis of the attitude towards foreign products confirms the existence of significant differences between countries.

Attitudes towards specific product categories

In our current study, focused on specific attitudes towards some product categories, we have found that *shoes* made in Spain are perceived, on a scale from 1 to 7, as follows (mean scores in brackets):

For Germans, they have a good appearance (5.0), reasonable price (4.9) and modern design (4.9). French consumers considered that Spanish shoes have wide variety (5.3), give a satisfactory result (5.2), have a good appearance (5.0) and are for the lower classes. Spanish respondents thought that Spanish shoes have a good appearance (5.9), are reliable (5.7) and well finished (5.6). Amongst the British respondents, Spanish shoes obtained intermediate values and they only emphasise good appearance (4.7). To sum up, we can consider that good appearance is the key cue for Spanish shoes, useful in a fashion product category. Consequently the strategic promotion effort must be directed towards emphasising this external attribute of Spanish shoes. Hardly any negative attributes appear, except the French perception 'of lower classes', so prices must be aimed at offering good value for money in this market.

For Spanish *toys* we found that for Germans there is not a clear attitude except good appearance (4.6). French consumers considered that Spanish toys have good appearance (4.8), offer a wide variety (4.8) and give a satisfactory result (4.7). Spaniards view their own toys as having good appearance (5.8), wide variety (5.6), modern design (5.2) and high prices (5.2). Again in this product category, the British view of Spanish toys was neutral, like in Germany, so a great effort must be made to promote Spanish toys among British and German consumers by communicating their benefits. These markets are of great importance because their per capita expenditure on toys is higher than Spain's. From an overall perspective, good appearance is the most valuable attribute on which advertising campaigns for toys could be based, but a pan-European campaign must be preceded by national campaigns in Germany and the United Kingdom. As Alden, Steenkamp & Batra (1999) point out, both positioning strategies could be used in different markets.

For Spanish *holiday resorts*, we found that Germans perceived them as attentive to their customers (5), with a good reputation (5) and with good appearance (5). French respondents considered that Spanish holiday resorts have advanced facilities (5.4), are competent (5.3), with a good reputation (5.1), with good appearance (5.1) and reliable (5). For the British, Spanish holiday resorts are attentive to the customers (4.6) and for the lower classes. In summary, Spanish holiday resorts must communicate service quality and individualised attention. It is obvious that one of the main objectives will be to work to achieve high levels of service in terms of customers' needs, but it is especially important at service encounter when the buyer-seller exchange takes place and when value is created for the customers. Promoting this attribute must be managed with caution due to consumer expectations. Creating a high level of expectation of personalised service could lead to a discrepancy between perceptions and expectations and finally the effect could become negative for companies within the tourist sector. One dimension to note is the perception held by the British that Spanish holiday resorts are 'for the lower classes'. This attitude may be associated with mass destinations, but is also affected by service quality.

For Spanish *oranges*, we found that Germans considered that they have prestige (5.7), high quality (5.5), reasonable prices (5.2) and are reliable (5). French respondents considered them to be naturally ripened (5.9) and of high quality (5.8). Spaniards think that their oranges are reliable (6.2), of high quality (6), guaranteed healthy (5.9) and have prestige (5.8). The British considered that Spanish oranges have high quality (4.6) and a reasonable price (4.6). We can consider that the most appreciated attributes are high quality and reasonable price. Both are positively related. Usually consumers perceive high prices with high quality. For Spanish oranges high quality is not absolutely related with high price. This evident competitive advantage must be the key dimension to be promoted for a pan-European campaign based on messages that highlight these two positive features. The country of origin cue represents a good basis for marketing Spanish oranges.

Finally we studied Spanish *wine*, and we found that Germans considered that Spanish wine has prestige (5.4), high quality (5.2), is produced by craftsmen (5.1) and reliable (5). French consumers perceived Spanish wine as follows: produced by

11

Preference	France	Germany	Spain	UK
Foreign	5.0	4.0	1.0	4.0
Indifferent	51.0	33.0	21.0	55.0
National	44.0	63.0	78.0	41.0

Table 2. Generic preference for national products (%)

craftsmen (6.1), additive free (5.9) and guaranteed to be healthy (5.9). Spaniards considered Spanish wine as reliable (6), guaranteed to be healthy (6), well bottled (6) and of high quality (5.9). For the British, Spanish wine has high quality (4.7) and prestige (4.6). The world currently produces more wine than it can consume, creating an urgent need to identify customers' needs and to fulfil them. An appropriate strategic orientation has been developed for wine companies (Lages & Shaw, 1999) and country of origin plays an important role for established producers. France as a major producer is an important competitor for Spanish wines. Consequently Spanish strategy in France must be different from that in other countries. From the data obtained we can conclude that Germans and British perceived Spanish wines as being of high quality, even better in Germany than in Britain. This quality attribute could be the basis of the advertising message for both countries, but this will not be enough to compete against French wines, and further research must be conducted to explore new ways of identifying more clear competitive advantages of Spanish wines over French ones.

General and specific preferences

Having seen the specific attitudes towards some Spanish products, let us now look at generic preferences in the countries included in our study.

In order to find out the general degree of preference of each sample for the products of its own country, a question was introduced to reflect this national feeling. The data is recorded in Table 2. We found that there is a significant difference among countries in their preference for national products over foreign ones.

Preference	France	Germany	Spain	UK
Refrigerators	France	Germany	Spain	Germany
Footwear	France	Italy	Spain	Italy
Toys	France	Germany	Spain	US
Banks	France	Germany	Spain	UK
Tourist Resorts	France	France	Not included	Spain
Oranges	Spain	Spain	Spain	Spain
Wines	France	France	Spain	France
Cheeses	France	France	Spain	France

Table 3. Summary of preferences by country

On considering each sub-sample, we observe that among Spaniards, 78% of the population prefer home products while 21% are indifferent. Germans prefer their own products (63%) and 33% are indifferent. In the French sample, 44% prefer their own products and 51% are indifferent. Among the British, 41% of the population prefer home products and 55% are indifferent. On comparing the percentages of each sub-sample we observe that the national feeling is more manifest among Spaniards, followed by Germans. An appreciable percentage of indifferent respondents appear in France and Britain.

A summary of product preferences by countries for specific categories is shown in Table 3. In this part we allowed respondents to mention other countries such as Italy and the USA, and other product categories, including the five analysed in the previous section and three more: refrigerators, banks and cheeses. Table 3 shows the country preference for every product category we considered.

From the results in Table 3, we can conclude that:

- The French and Spanish show higher preference for their own products.
- In services, such as banks, each country prefers its own, due to the effect of confidence.
- Spain is preferred for oranges in all countries. Spain has a weak position in footwear and toys. The preferences of respondents for shoes show different results. Thus while French and Spanish respondents prefer their own country's shoes, these same products are not preferred in Germany and Britain, where Italian shoes are the most highly preferred. The influence of national feeling is even more in evidence in relation to toys. It thus seems as though there is a poor acquaintance with toy products made outside the home country, or that there is no clear influence of the 'made in' effect.
- France is Spain's strongest competitor in tourist resorts, wines and cheeses. Spaniards prefer their own wines and cheeses while the British, Germans and French prefer French ones. In conclusion, it can be said that French wines and cheeses occupy a high place in the preferences of consumers in the countries analysed, except in Spain. Spanish tourist resorts are preferred by the British, and French tourist resorts by Germans and French. A previous study conducted only in Britain and Spain (Miquel, Bigné & Newman, 1993) showed the same pattern as the current study in country preferences for shoes and wines.

One of the objectives of our study was to measure consumer ethnocentrism with the CETSCALE. In Table 4 we can see some results showing the ethnocentrism of each

	France	Germany	Spain	UK
Mean of the scale	62.3	52.8	80.1	53.1
Standard deviation	18.6	20.7	19.0	14.0
Mean of the items	3.6	3.1	4.7	3.1

Table 4. Consumer Ethnocentrism on the basis of the CETSCALE.

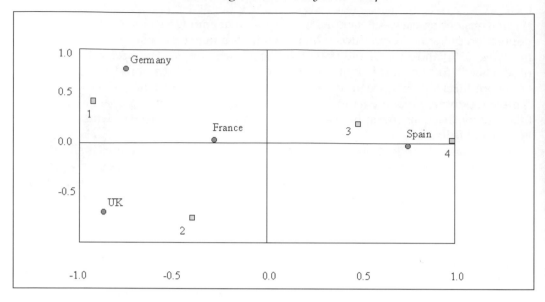

Map 1. Consumer ethnocentrism

country. The data suggests that Spain is the most ethnocentric country, followed by France, the UK and Germany with similar data. We obtain significant differences between Spain and France/the UK/Germany; between France and the UK/Germany, but not between the UK and Germany. So, British and German consumers share a similar level of ethnocentricity.

A more graphic presentation of these results can be seen in the next map. We have

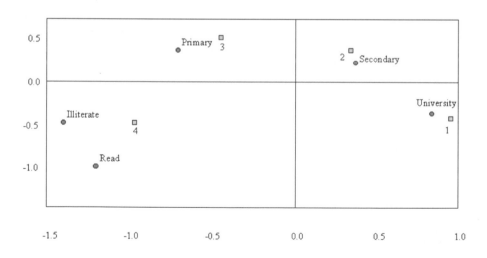

Map 2. Relationship between studies and consumer ethnocentrism

divided the ethnocentrism belief into four levels from 1 to 4, and we used a correspondence factor analysis to obtain the maps referred to in this chapter.

We measured the influence of some moderating factors on consumer ethnocentrism and we found only a positive relation between ethnocentrism and age. Conversely, there is a negative relationship between ethnocentrism and educational level, income, cultural openness, travel abroad, foreign restaurants visited and knowledge of languages.

As can be seen on Map 2, people with university education are close to level 1, the lowest level of ethnocentricity, and the illiterate are close to level 4.

Conclusions

Published research seems to suggest the existence, though controversial to some, of an influence of the country of manufacture of a product on the image of that product. Throughout this study we have aimed to analyse the relationship between the image of the country of manufacture and the preferences of consumers for its products. This relationship, known as the 'country of origin' or 'made in' effect, has been the subject of many papers and studies; few, however, have been carried out among countries belonging to the European Union where the flow of trade exchanges is high and will in the future tend to grow in importance.

We focused on various categories of products made in different European countries, for British, French, German and Spanish samples.

Regarding the specific objectives of this study, the main conclusions reached are as follows:

- Country of origin effect is a valuable cue for Spanish products only in specific product categories.
- In general, there is not a bad attitude towards Spanish products, but only some attributes emerge as positive.
- Agricultural products are the most highly preferred.
- Spaniards show high ethnocentrism compared with the UK and Germany.

The measurement of overall preference for products made in the respondent's own country shows a preference for the national products amongst the Spanish and German samples and a moderate preference amongst the British and French samples.

References

Alden, D.L., Steenkamp, J-B.E.M. & Batra, R., 'Brand Positioning Through Advertising in Asia, North America, and Europe: The Role of Global Consumer Culture', *Journal of Marketing*, 63: January 1999, pp. 75–87.

Babb, H., Lascuand, D.N. & Vann, E., 'Personality Traits and Country-of-Origin Cues: Evaluating Consumer Predisposition to seek Country-of-Origin Information' in *Proceedings of the Sixth Biannual World Marketing Congress*, pp. 451–455, Istanbul: Academy of Marketing Science, 1993.

Bannister, J.P. & Saunders, J.A., 'UK Consumers' Attitudes towards Imports: The Measurement of National Stereotype Image', *European Journal of Marketing*, 12:8 (1978), pp. 562–70.

Bigné, E., Miquel, S. & Newman, K., 'La imagen de los productos fabricados en España'. *Información Comercial Española*, 722: octubre 1993, pp. 49–60.

Bilkey, W.T. & Nes, E., 'Country-of-Origin Effects on Product Evaluations', *Journal of International Business Studies*, 13:1 (1982), pp. 89–99.

Bozell-Gallup, 'Liga mundial de la calidad', *IPMARK*, 426: 16-31 de marzo 1994, pp. 30–32.

Cattin, P., Jolibert, A. & Lohnes, C., 'A Cross Cultural Study of "Made-in" Concepts', *Journal of International Business Studies*, 13:3 (1982), pp. 131–41.

Cicic, M., Tsai, J.J. & Patterson, P.G., 'Country-of-Origin Effect for Taiwanese-made Personal Computer Products in Australia' in *Proceedings of the Sixth Biannual World Marketing Congress*, pp. 402–5, Istanbul: Academy of Marketing Science, 1993.

Cordell, V.V., 'Effects on Consumer Preferences for Foreign-sourced Products', *Journal of International Business Studies*, 23:2 (1992), pp. 251–69.

Chao, P., 'The Impact of Country Affiliation on the Credibility of Products' Attribute Claims', *Journal of Advertising Research*, 29:2 (1989), pp. 35–42.

D'Astous, A. & Ahmed, S.A., 'Country-of-Origin Effects as a Function of Personality Variables' in *Proceedings of the Sixth Biannual World Marketing Congress*. pp. 447–50, Istanbul: Academy of Marketing Science, 1993.

Erickson, G.M., Johansson, J.K. & Chao, P., 'Images Variables in Multi-Attribute Product Evaluations: Country-of-Origin Effects', *Journal of Consumer Research*, 11: September 1984, pp. 694–99.

Eroglu, S.A. & Machleit, K.A., 'Effects of Individual and Product-Specific Variables on Utilising Country-of-Origin as a Product Quality Cue', *International Marketing Review*, 6:6 (1989), pp. 27–41.

Ettenson, R & Gaeth, G., 'Consumers Perceptions of Hybrid (Bi-National) Products', *Journal of Consumer Marketing*, 8: Fall 1991, pp. 13–18.

Etzel, M.J. & Walker, B.J., 'Advertising Strategy for Foreign Products', *Journal of Advertising Research*, 14:3 (1974), pp. 41–4.

Han, C.M., 'Country Image: Halo or Summary Construct?', *Journal of Marketing Research*, 26:2 (1989), pp. 222–9.

Han, C.M. & Terpstra, V., 'Country-of-Origin Effects for Uni-National and Bi-National Products', *Journal of International Business Studies*, 19:2 (1988), pp. 235–56.

Johansson, J., Douglas, S. & Nonaka, I., 'Assessing the Impact of Country-of-Origin on Product Evaluations: A New Methodological Perspective', *Journal of Marketing Research*, 22:4 (1985), pp. 388–96.

Kaynak, E. & Kucukemiroglu, O., 'Sourcing of Industrial Products: Regiocentric Orientation of Chinese Organizational Buyers', *European Journal of Marketing*, 26:5 (1992), pp. 36–55.

Kaynak, E. & Cavusgil, S.T., 'Consumer Attitudes towards products of foreign origin: Do they vary across product classes?', *International Journal of Advertising*, 2:2 (1983), pp. 147–57.

Lages, L.F. & Shaw, V. 'The marketing strategies for Port Wine Companies', *International Journal of Wine Marketing*, 10:2 (1999), pp. 5–23.

Minor, M. & Hodges, D., 'Country-of-Origin Effects on Product Preferences: A Flexible Regression Analysis' in *Proceedings of the Annual Conference of the Academy of Marketing Science. Developments in Marketing Science*, vol XVI, pp. 203–7, Miami Beach, Florida: AMS, 1993.

Miquel, S., Bigné, E. & Newman, K., 'Buying Preference and Positioning in Spain and Britain of Products made in Various European Countries' in *Proceedings of the 22nd European Marketing Academy Conference*, vol 2, pp. 935–54, Barcelona: EMAC, 1993.

Miquel, S., Newman, K., Bigné, E. & Chansarkar, B., 'Aspects of Anglo-Spanish Perceptions and Product Preferences arising from Country-of-Origin Image', *International Journal of Advertising*, 12:2 (1993), pp. 131–42.

Nagashima, A., 'A Comparative "Made-in" Product Image Survey among Japanese Businessmen', *Journal of Marketing*, 41: July 1977, pp. 95–100.

Netemeyer, R.G., Durvasula, S. & Lichtenstein, D.R., 'A Cross-National Assessment of the Reliability and Validity of the CETSCALE', *Journal of Marketing Research*, XXVIII: August 1991, pp. 320–7.

Papadopoulos, N. & Heslop, L.A. (Eds). Product Country Images: Impact and their Role in International Marketing, New York: The Haworth Press, 1993.

Pecotich, A., Pressley, M. & Roth, D., 'The Impact of Ethnocentrism on the Country-of-Origin Effect in the Service Sector' in *Proceedings of the 22nd European Marketing Academy Conference*, vol 2, pp. 1245–57, Barcelona: EMAC, 1993.

Peterson, R.A. & Jolibert, A.J.P., 'A Meta-analysis of Country-of-Origin Effects', *Journal of International Business Studies*, 26:4 (1995), pp. 883–900.

Sharma, S., Shimp, T. & Shin, J., 'Consumer Ethnocentrism: A Test of Antecedents and Moderators', *Journal of the Academy of Marketing Science*, 23:1 (1995), pp. 26–37.

Shimp, T. & Sharma, S., 'Consumer Ethnocentrism: Construction and Validation of the CETSCALE', *Journal of Marketing Research*, 27: August 1987, pp. 280–9.

Wall, M., Liefeld, J. & Heslop, L.A., 'Impact of Country-of-Origin Cue on Consumer Judgements in Multi-Cue Situations: a Covariance Analysis', *Journal of the Academy of Marketing Science*, 19:2 (1991), pp. 105–13.

White, P.D. & Cundiff, E.W., 'Assessing the Quality of Industrial Products', *Journal of Marketing*, 42:1 (1978), pp. 80–5.

2   Supra-Nationality and Sub-Nationality in Spanish Advertising

Jackie Cannon
Oxford Brookes University

In an earlier study (Cannon, 1998), I explored a number of factors which have contributed to Spain's inability to define a strong national image for its products, analysing such aspects as economic development, recent historico-political events, reliance on foreign technology, entrepreneurial practices and the internationalisation of industry. The slogan of Catalan industrialists 'hacer empresa es hacer país' (the making of a company is the making of a country), used in the early twentieth century, would, at first sight, seem to be evidence of a will to define a national image for industrial production at the time and yet, in reality, there is still little evidence of positive attitudes to Spanish products. A review of some of the advertising practices used by Spanish companies is, therefore, valuable in order to understand why they have apparently had relatively little success in projecting a positive national image for their products.

Reflecting the country of origin

In a global market, the lack of a national image may not be important. Indeed, given how difficult it can be to determine the nationality of products that are branded by a company of one nationality, manufactured in another country and then marketed all over the world, one could argue that national associations contribute little or nothing to the product identity. However, precisely because of the rapid impact needed from advertising, the fact that we find such associations being used would seem to indicate a belief on the part of advertisers that such associations do serve a purpose.

We can start by reviewing a number of strategies employed by advertisers to identify links with nationality as a means of highlighting positive product attributes. Language is one tool which is variously employed to transmit a message about nationality. One finds some companies, such as Audi VW, using a slogan written in German in advertisements in the British press, leaving the consumer with little doubt as to the nationality of the product. The same practice is also found with the use of English in foreign journals when advertising some British products. Another way of confirming nationality is by the inclusion of written statements which ensure that the reader is conscious of the origin of the product by directly stating it, as in the case of the slogan used by AEG, the German white goods manufacturer, 'Advanced Engineering from Germany', using the same acronym for the slogan as for the name of the company (Allgemeine Elektricitäts-Gesellschaft). Likewise, Swiss watchmakers frequently include the words Switzerland or Genève in their ads. Another, more subtle way of conveying nationality as a positive product attribute is the symbolic use of the national flag or at least the colours of the national flag.

Further study reveals that nationality in product advertising is often used in a way which transmits an ambiguous message about the place of origin, at times appropriating one nation's traditions and values into the marketing strategies of a company from another country. This strategy is employed when the attitudes of foreign consumers are expected to be more positive towards a particular product/country combination. An example of this is Mássimo Dutti, a Spanish fashion designer and retailer, but whose name is misleading, seeming Italian rather than Spanish. This slight deception is understandable given the perceived link between Italy, fashion and style. The Spanish porcelain company, Lladró, also employs these tactics in Britain by advertising their figurines accompanied by a short text from Keats' poetry, reminiscent of Victorian heritage in Britain, in order to reinforce the nostalgic values embodied by their products. A further example of marketing strategies which transmit ambiguous messages about the country of origin is found in the advertising of the Spanish car manfacturer, SEAT, which has not had the opportunity to present a positive image due to State intervention policies aimed at protecting national industry and the domestic market and, later, due to the amount of foreign investment in this sector. The positive values used in advertisements when VW became a major shareholder of SEAT in the 1980s were not attributed to Spain, highlighting instead German engineering and Mediterranean design. A similar example, this time of the Mediterranean, rather than Spain, being used to promote a product is the ad for Codorníu sparkling wine with the text 'Nacido en el Mediterráneo'. There are no additional clues which would link the product to Spain.

One can also find examples of text written in English which uses an alternative typeface which mimics, for example, Japanese pictograms, thereby reinforcing positive perceptions towards electronic goods produced in Japan. Such uses can be effectively exploited by advertisers of non-Japanese products disguising the true country of origin while aiming to capitalise on any unconscious positive associations that may be triggered in the receiver of an advertisement.

Another technique is to make use of cultural symbols which are easily recognisable and can reinforce positive qualities of products according to their country of origin. Examples of this are commonly found in advertisements for tourist destinations in the British press. We find an increasing number of advertisements which combine a number of different ways of facilitating the prompt recognition of a destination or product origin. One characteristic of these types of associations is the growing tendency to blur the message to the extent that it is at times difficult to be sure which product is being advertised. Either there is a certain ambiguity relating to what is really being advertised or there is a deliberate attempt to combine a number of popular symbols in one advertisement to strengthen the impact of each of the advertisers.

Two further examples of location being incorporated into advertising strategies can be observed in some European advertising. Geographical delimitations of regions are sometimes employed to enhance perceived quality attributes or we may also find that supra-national references are used. A review of a single edition of an Italian magazine (*L'Espresso*, 1999) revealed three examples of the European label being used, firstly with reference to the Carta Club Eurostar train service, then for Indesit refrigerators accompanied by subtitles in English saying 'Made in Europe' and 'Leader for young Europe', and finally, for the furniture manufacturer, Gruppo Euromobil, whose name indicates its origin because of the spelling. In all of these cases, the familiar blue of the European flag and a representation of the symbolic ring of stars are featured. In addition, the association with the symbol of the post-national era of a united Europe is used in a way which is deemed to provoke positive attitudes.

The emergence of the European Union or any other collective of countries creates triggers which evoke sub-national or supra-national distinguishing features. Examples of the use of regional characteristics and symbols being used in the marketing of products can be found in printed magazines in a number of countries, even if the subject is not explicit and the country of origin not specifically mentioned. Images of mist-shrouded hillsides might accompany a picture of a whisky bottle in Britain, evoking distinguishing northern climatic and topographical features. A wizened old hag clothed in mourning black will encourage the viewer to make an association with the best of traditional Mediterranean cooking. Mountain scenes in Spanish advertising can depict sun or cloud, depending on which part of the country is being highlighted; Andalusia's mountains are photographed for tourism adverts to promote skiing; and the Zoco Pacharán liqueur producers in the north of Spain prefer images of autumnal, misty copses which embody the key features of freshness and naturalness they wish to promote. Neither campaign would be immediately recognisable to many foreigners as representing Spanish products and regions, particularly if the readers were only familiar with the sun, sea and sand stereotype. However, it is worth noting that the Zoco advertisement referred to here is printed in the Spanish press and would receive a different interpretation amongst Spaniards. This would depend on how appealing the associations were to them, something which in turn would be likely to be influenced by their own level of familiarity with the area portrayed as well as their willingness to interpret regional connections and thereby endow the product with a positive regional identity.

The theories offered by some political scientists (Willis, 1996) about the motivation behind highlighting regional qualities, and in this way constructing identities, can offer some useful insights into the possible influences on entrepreneurial practices, indicating as Willis points out, that regional collective identity is constructed from political interests and the context of particular actors seeking to develop a myth of regional identity. This notion can be easily understood in the context of Catalan bourgeois industrialists and those in other regions of Spain with a claim to historical nationality.

Due largely to its problematic and tardy evolution, the industrial sector in Spain has had great difficulties in identifying aspects which can be readily and positively perceived by the potential consumer. However, Spain's late development is not the only reason why Spanish goods do not enjoy a high-quality image. The projected image, it is argued here, is influenced by how Spaniards react to their historical context and view themselves, resulting in a widespread reluctance to rely on national attributes. A fuller understanding of this assertion depends on examining a number of cultural factors relating to identity.

Regional identity in Spain

It is true that international brands cannot be formed when the country is not able to develop international markets but, due mainly to its natural resources and climatic factors, Spain did, and still does, depend largely on potential clients visiting the tourist resorts in order to become familiar with Spanish products. Yet, while the business sector in countries in the now developed world were developing their industries and establishing an often country-specific identity for their exported products, the Spanish business sector was concentrating on the national market. At the time that neighbouring European countries were building their industries, Spain was struggling with political conflicts, many of which were to persist long after the end of the Franco regime.

One of the strongest sources of opposition to the dictatorship was the desire for regional devolution driven by the strength of identity felt in the 'nacionalidades históricas' (Hooper,1987). Indeed, one of the first issues to be tackled by the central government during the transition period was the granting of statutes of autonomy to regions whose roots were not in a united Spain but in a distinct regional identity based on historical, linguistic and cultural heritage. The different trajectories of the distinct regions in the last twenty-five years in Spain have been traced by economists, historians, linguists and political scientists, amongst others, but the contribution made by sociologists to the debate on how Spanish industry has developed is less widely recorded. In his study of national attitudes, the Spanish sociologist, Amando de Miguel (1990) concludes that 'Definitivamente, lo nuestro es no entendernos' (we are very good at not understanding each other). Within this context the role of regional identity has to be considered as a contributory factor in the lack of will to develop a national image.

What is apparent from the many and wide-ranging studies of Spain's recent history is that claims for regional recognition have shaped many policies and generated many rivalries between the regions. While not ignoring factors such as government economic policy and foreign investment, one can argue that pride in regional heritage has, at least in the case of Spain, limited the will on the part of the business community to promote a national image for its products if the nation in question is Spain, or the Spanish State as many prefer to call it, thus detaching themselves from a centrally-governed entity. The history of the country with its suppression of regional identities, its inward-looking economic policies and its lack of political progress became a feature that many Spaniards were keener to forget than promote. The eagerness with which Spain embraced the European Union reflected a belief that Europe represented something better than existed at home.

The feeling that Europe was superior was identified in 1996 in a study published by the Spanish Ministry of Trade and Tourism (MCT,1996) in which it was stated that Spaniards generally held a poorer view of themselves than foreigners did, generally believing that Spanish quality is inferior to foreign quality. However, one has to distinguish between perceptions which relate to the country and its geography, quality of the workforce and recognition of cultural heritage in addition to perceptions held about products. We find that, while Spanish culture, for example, is viewed positively, the 'made in Spain' label for manufactured products does not appear to embody positive values for those outside Spain. The report commissioned by the Spanish Ministry finds that Europeans always express a preference for a non-Spanish product over a Spanish product with the same characteristics. For historical reasons relating to the development of industry and advertising in Spain it is not surprising that Europeans prefer German white goods or British jeans ahead of these products from Spain. However, the fact that, as noted in the MCT report (paragraph 19.2.7), Italian olive oil is preferred to Spanish would indicate that the image has a lot to do with the style or amount of advertising both within Spain and in international markets.

The internationalisation of Spain's economy came principally from foreign direct investment in Spanish industry and this has resulted in a lack of familiarity with Spanish products abroad. Marketing specialists refer to the role of the 'pull' factor – presence in another country of one exporting company retaining its local suppliers who then become exporters – and affirm that it is a key factor in company internationalisation. Explanations for such activity can be found in the work of Porter (1990), amongst others, but it must be noted that Spain's industrial development did not stimulate such a phenomenon as very few companies dared to enter the international arena, being traditionally risk-averse in such markets.

It is not surprising then that the level of familiarity amongst foreigners with Spanish products is not good, and the fact that Spaniards appear to share this view makes it a far more acceptable strategy to either hide or disguise the Spanish origin of products. The Italian-sounding Mássimo Dutti company name; SEAT's design adverts, albeit as a result of a German company's policy; the use of Keats' poetry for porcelain; and the 'Born in the Mediterranean' text accompanying Codorníu's Cava, would all appear to support this view. The common element, however, shared by all these companies is that they all originate in regions which are noted for the strength of their anti-centralist attitudes. SEAT, albeit originally a State company, was founded in Barcelona; Codorníu is produced by the descendants of a noted Catalan family; Lladró, similarly, is of Valencian stock and Mássimo Dutti was established in Galicia. The reluctance of certain companies to identify themselves as Spanish is more understandable in this framework.

While the use of the nation as an identifying feature may be relatively unpopular, the tendency to use the term 'Mediterranean' invites one to consider the values that this notion embodies in order to understand its positive contribution to marketing strategy.

What constitutes 'Mediterranean'?
Historically, the Mediterranean Sea was at the centre of the known world, delimiting the boundaries and providing a maritime highway for the Greeks, Phoenicians, Venetians and Crusaders and becoming, as a result, the source of economic prosperity in surrounding regions.

In geographic terms, 'Mediterranean' necessarily incorporates those countries or regions which border the sea of the same name, including North Africa and some Balkan countries whose shores, although they have shorelines on seas with other names, such as Aegean, Adriatic, Tyrrhenian and Ligurian, are in effect washed by the same body of water.

In a geo-political context, the validity of the concept is debatable. Mediterranean countries do not constitute a political unit. To inhabitants of the EU, Mediterranean countries are usually understood to be those of Southern Europe bordered by the sea. However, this definition rarely includes France, and where France is represented as Mediterranean, it does not imply the whole country but only certain southern regions of the country. Recognising the distinction between the industrial north of France and the agricultural south may allow us to approach an understanding of the concept of Mediterranean. In addition to this, we have further evidence from the EU that 'Mediterranean' is not a reflection of geographical position given that policies which focus on Mediterranean economic needs are often understood to include Portugal. So France is not a Mediterranean country but Portugal is.

The above could imply a pejorative view of 'Mediterranean' as 'underdeveloped', yet we can find examples of Mediterranean being used to describe the positive features of olives and various other fruits and vegetables and the terms 'Mediterranean cuisine' or 'Mediterranean diet' are frequently encountered. This use of 'Mediterranean' is common enough for us to believe that it has a clear and recognisable identity. Much is being made of this in Spain, with local governments currently promoting healthy eating, particularly amongst school-aged children, under the Mediterranean umbrella. Is it reasonable to assume, then, that Mediterranean is synonymous with agricultural or less industrialised, and therefore in need of special economic consideration?

Since there is no political unity nor a clear geographic definition, perhaps the explanation should be sought in other connotations of the term Mediterranean, which are presumably positive. If it is not merely locational, political or sectorial, to what extent can we identify what does constitute Mediterranean and why is it that some manufacturers in Spain choose to use this association in preference to the more definable one of nationality?

The most simple explanation is undoubtedly the fact that Spanish products do not enjoy a very positive image. Nevertheless, the attitude of Spaniards towards the Mediterranean is generally positive as images of water in a country frequently blighted by drought are understandably likely to stimulate positive reactions. It is logical that the Mediterranean should be associated with relaxation and holidays in a country whose population heads to the coast for the entire month of August. Even though patterns of tourism are changing, many of those who live in Madrid or anywhere to the south-east, east or north-east of the capital, will spend their holidays in or near a Mediterranean resort. Even if one is referring not to a coastal resort but to a nearby location, the idea of proximity is crucial as many Spaniards would assert that the characteristically whitewashed buildings of small towns in Andalusia reflect the essence of the Mediterranean, despite being, in some cases, closer to the Atlantic Ocean.

Of course, the adjective 'Mediterranean' does describe the sea and the beach, but is not restricted to these physical features. It is also used to describe people and their temperament, exemplified in the words of Hilaire Belloc: 'The most degraded of them all Mediterranean we call. His hair is crisp, and even curls, And he is saucy with the girls' (*Penguin Dictionary of Quotations*, 1980). This is not a description of Spaniards as such, but would be understood by many North Europeans as being applicable to Spaniards, Greeks and Italians alike. Arguably, one of the most wide-ranging and comprehensive descriptions of the Mediterranean character and lifestyle as understood by a Spaniard can be found in the words to the song 'Mediterráneo' by Joan Manuel Serrat, in which he makes no apologies for having a wild seafarer's soul which enjoys wine and song, while employing the traditional images associated with the seaside and playing in the sand:

> Soy cantor, soy embustero,
> me gusta el juego y el vino.
> Tengo alma de marinero...
> Qué le voy a hacer, si yo
> nací en el Mediterráneo.

It is important to remember, however, that interpretations of the Mediterranean are likely to differ greatly according to the potential consumer's location when the image is triggered. Tourists from other parts of Europe may well arrive *en masse* in Spain with a preconceived idea of what Mediterranean represents, but in Spain understanding of the term is not restricted to memories of holidays but encompasses a wider range of associations. While it is the case that many Spaniards spend their holidays on this particular coast, they have a greater awareness than foreigners of the political geography of the country, recognising that Catalonia and Valencia, two of the most prosperous regions with their own regional language, extend along the Mediterranean coast of the whole eastern territory of Spain. If natives of Madrid go to either of these two regions for their Mediterranean vacation, they will be required to read road signs, menus and a range of other instructions in a language which is not their mother tongue, thereby experiencing some of the excitement (or discomfort) linked to foreign travel while remaining in their own country. Given that the Catalans and the Valencians have chosen to promote their Mediterranean coast in the regional language, as 'Mediterrània', the term may be deemed to embody a range of product attributes extending beyond the product itself and incorporating other elements of brand identity such as service quality and differentiation from the competition. Likewise, Murcia has carved out a distinct identity by naming its stretch of coast the Costa Cálida, while Andalusia has retained the Costa del Sol label.

The Mediterranean, of course, does not belong exclusively to Spain. The term constitutes a marketing tool which conveniently allows some manufacturers to make associations with a supra-national entity. In addition, Spain's membership of the European Union facilitates the incorporation of positive features linked to a supra-national body in the identification of its products. A recent example of this strategy is the new Euromed train service which, like its Italian Eurostar counterpart referred to earlier, is not featuring nationality but is making use of both the Mediterranean and the European labels as well as adopting a name which does not betray its origins, sounding as if it could come from any part of Europe. While it is true that the service has a link across the Pyrennees, it is another example of the Spanish preference for oblique national frontiers and identifying with European, rather than Spanish, characteristics. In this way, they can attempt to shut the door on a heritage best forgotten in the minds of many.

Conclusion

Perceptions of identifiable national characteristics and expertise are a useful tool in advertising, highlighting, for example, fashion from Italy, engineering from Germany and precision from Switzerland. However, one finds Spanish companies avoiding this strategy and evoking British Victorian nostalgia, disguising the country of origin and defining their products according to regional subdivisions. Within this context, the subregion of the Mediterranean appears to have a widely, if not unanimously accepted identity and in Spain it appears that whatever constitutes this identity, whether it be lifestyle, relaxation, or quality, it is at least preferable to being defined in national terms. In all the examples we have seen of Spanish products being marketed with the European, Mediterranean or regional labels, we can find one common feature: the companies could have used the word Spanish in their advertising but instead the non-national adjective is used as a way of emphasising regional differences and avoiding the association with the nation-state.

The political context in which Spanish industry has evolved both during and since the Franco era has shaped the enthusiasm with which Europe is viewed and the pride in regional heritage in Spain. The emergence of sub-national and supra-national entities has allowed some sectors to make use of icons and other cultural associations which transcend national frontiers or allow the historical 'sub-nations' to flourish, thereby minimising the impact of regional hostilities in the interests of commercial progress and regional differentiation. Maybe, then, we have to understand the 'país' to which the Catalan industrialists referred as something other than the nation-state, being rather more likely to be the historic Basque Country or *Els Països Catalans* and *El País Valencià*, as they are defined in their respective regional languages.

References

Belloc, H., *Ladies and Gentlemen*, 'The Three Races' as quoted in *The Penguin Dictionary of Quotations*, London: Penguin, 1980.

Cannon, J., 'Spain as a marketing tool: an examination of perceptions of Spanish products', *International Journal of Iberian Studies*, 11:2 (1998).

de Miguel, A., *Los Españoles*, 2nd edn, Madrid: Ediciones Temas de Hoy, 1990.

Hooper, J., *The Spaniards*, 2nd edn, London: Penguin, 1987.

L'Espresso, 22 July 1999.

Ministerio de Comercio y Turismo, La imagen exterior de España: Aspectos comerciales, turísticos e inversores, Madrid: 1996.

Porter, Michael E., *The Competitive Advantage of Nations*, London: Macmillan, 1990.

Willis, D., 'When East goes West: The Political Economy of European Integration in the Post-Cold War Era' in Wintle, M. (ed.) *Culture and Identity in Europe*, London: Ashgate Publishing, 1996.

3 'Danes don't tell lies'

On the Place of 'Made In' Advertising in a Post-National Trading Environment

David Head
University of Northumbria at Newcastle

Back in 1988, with the creation of a frontierless European single market in the offing, I put forward the view, in an article for the *International Journal of Advertising*, that 'nation-oriented selling-points' not only had an undeniable part to play in the marketing process, but might even become an increasingly attractive advertising strategy as the single European market 'spreads its mantle of national anonymity over products and services being proffered by each member state to the others' (Head, 1988). Not long after that, Porter (1990:19) concluded that 'while globalization of competition might appear to make the nation less important, instead it makes it more so: with fewer impediments to trade to shelter uncompetitive domestic firms and industries, the home nation takes on growing significance because it is the source of the skills and technology that underpin competitive advantage'.

This suggested that the paradox I perceived in the case of country-of-origin advertising, which seemed likely to flourish in a frontierless trading environment, might be an expression of some prime economic phenomenon. 'Companies, at first glance, seem to have transcended countries', observed Porter (1990:18–19), but he claimed that 'differences in national economic structures, values, cultures, institutions, and histories contribute profoundly to competitive success'.

Just twelve years after my article appeared, the single European market has firmly established itself as an everyday reality and eleven member states have committed themselves to a single European currency. It therefore seems to be a good time to test my theory. I do so by telling a tale of two *Der Spiegels*, one from a key date in 1990, and one covering momentous events in 1999.

On 1 October 1990, *Der Spiegel* carried an advertisement for the Danish-made Dynaudio speakers which asked the question: 'Where are Germans lied to most frequently?' ('Wo werden die Deutschen am häufigsten angelogen?'). This appeared under the picture of a bed and was followed by a long statement which began by claiming that the Germans will believe almost anything, for instance that empires last a thousand years, that nuclear power stations are completely safe and that they (the Germans) set the standard when it comes to the horizontal arts ('Den Deutschen kann man so ziemlich alles erzählen. Dass Reiche tausend Jahre währen, Kernkraftwerke völlig sicher sind und dass sie [die Deutschen] in der Horizontalen Weltstandard haben'). The advertisement claimed, on the other hand, that Danes 'love the truth', and it was the truth which came out of Dynaudio speakers, as befitted the brand of a company whose motto was: 'Danes don't tell lies' ('Dänen lügen nicht'). To underline this point graphically, the advertisement included a picture of the company's main lie-detector, the ear of chief quality controller Sven-Erik Nielsen.

The same issue of *Der Spiegel* also contained an advertisement for the Danish-made, gin-like drink Jubilaeums Akvavit, a glass of which is being held by a young woman in a cocktail dress who is depicted posing on a rock like Copenhagen's Little Mermaid statue and looking out across some trawlers, each one flying the Danish flag. The advertisement provides further assistance to the would-be purchaser with the explanation: 'A mermaid doesn't need much. A well-placed rock, some tangy sea air and her *Jubi*'. Just to make sure, it adds the slogan: 'Cool, soft, Danish' ('Kühl, sanft, dänisch'), which the company had been using in the German press since the mid-1980s.

However, this was the beginning of the 1990s, and the frontierless Single European Market was in the offing, a development which might be expected to diminish the value of 'country-of-origin' advertising. After all, in 1983, the European Commission had endorsed the view of the European Communities' Economic and Social Committee that a product's country of origin 'did not fill a genuine consumer need', whereas 'price, composition, grade, quality and instructions for use' were important, and in 1985 the Court of Justice of the European Communities had rejected the argument that consumer protection was safeguarded by compulsory indications of national origin, because consumers associated the quality of certain goods with the countries in which they were made (Head, 1988). Indeed, the Court believed that it was protectionism rather than consumer protection which was promoted by highlighting the national origin of products. For such a practice might prompt the consumer to give preference to certain national products and enable them to 'assert any prejudices which they may have against foreign products' (PCJEC, 1985). Of course, what we see in the shape of both the Single European Market and its ethos is globalisation in microcosm.

By 1990, the European Court's views were being echoed by the foremost exponent of the theory that globalisation was producing a world in which national differences no longer mattered to consumers. In *The Borderless World: Power and Strategy in the Interlinked Economy*, Kenichi Ohmae (1990:3) contended vigorously that in the new trading context, customers enjoyed a new power *vis-à-vis* manufacturers partly because of their 'lack of allegiances'. What Ohmae calls 'economic nationalism', he acknowledges, 'flourishes during election campaigns and infects what legislatures do and what particular interest groups ask for', but 'when individuals vote with their pocket-book – when they walk into a store or showroom anywhere in Europe, the United States, or Japan – they leave behind the rhetoric and mudslinging':

> Do you write with a Waterman or a Mt. Blanc pen or travel with a Vuitton suitcase out of nationalist sentiments? Probably not. You buy these things because they represent the kind of value you're looking for.
>
> At the cash register, you don't care about country of origin or country of residence. You don't think about employment figures or trade deficits. You don't worry about where

the product was made [...] What you care about most is the product's quality, price, design, value and appeal to you as a consumer.

Viewed in this context, the projection of the honest, cool, gentle Danish image in two full-page advertisements in *Der Spiegel* on 1 October 1990 appears to be anachronistic and a waste of money. However, the fact should not be overlooked that the European Court had, in the judgement referred to above, by implication recognised the power of country-of-origin associations in the minds of consumers in identifying the potential for discrimination against certain products on the grounds that they came from the 'wrong' place as far as purchasers were concerned. Furthermore, it had pointed out that 'if the national origin of goods brings certain qualities to the minds of consumers', it was 'in the manufacturers' interests to indicate it themselves on the goods or on their packaging' (PCJEC 1985). We could easily insert the phrase 'or in their advertising'. We might also argue that Kenichi Ohmae is overlooking the possibility that 'country-of-origin' factors could well contribute to the assessment of a product or to its appeal by way of association with notions of positive national – or even regional – attributes or reputations. It is therefore possibly not surprising that the same issue of *Der Spiegel* contained only one overtly European advertisement. This was a very small one for the congress centre in Freudenstadt under the slogan: 'Willkommen Europa' and a picture of the European flag being presented by two people who presumably work for the Centre. True, there was also a full-page advertisement for one of Germany's leading banks, the Bank für Gemeinwirtschaft (usually abbreviated to BfG and since January 2000 Swedish-owned) which highlighted the need for companies to get ready for the increase in competition that would come from completion of the Single European Market in 1993. But the graphic representation of the argument is a row of pencils each bearing the 'Made in' label of the then twelve member states directly affected by the 1993 deadline, from 'Made in Belgium' to 'Made in Spain'. Just as significantly, the advertisement also focused attention specifically on the boom being experienced by 'the German economy' and on the need to take into account the regional states then known as the 'new *Länder*', a post-unification reference to the former GDR.

The BfG advertisement was therefore concerned above all with the interests of Germany or rather of German firms on 1 October 1990 than on any impending Europeanisation of their image. On the face of it, this is very much in tune with the preoccupation of *Der Spiegel* on that date, just two days away from the completion of German unification. The cover page depicted an eagle bestriding the globe against the background of a German banknote and asking the question 'After unification – world power Germany?' ('Nach der Einheit – Weltmacht Deutschland?'). Furthermore, the main feature article on this theme demonstrates the 'sober' way in which Germany's business partners are sizing up the economic implications of unification by citing the Danes. According to the article, they had calculated the extent to which Denmark would benefit from the import boom in the newly opened ex-GDR market: 40,000 jobs and 5 billion Kroner, an insight evidently not lost on the Danish advertisers in this unification issue of *Der Spiegel*. The preoccupation of the day is duly the nation, and

28

the 'made in' advertisements contained in *Der Spiegel* on 1 October 1990 seem very much in line with this orientation:

- Viala wine from Yugoslavia, which in the context of this *Der Spiegel* seems uncannily prescient when one thinks of the way that country has been instrumental in placing Germany's military contribution to NATO beyond doubt.
- German film director Volker Schlöndorff sitting in a chair made by Vitra of Weil am Rhein, as the advertisement tells us.
- An advertisement depicting an Italian setting for the gin-like drink Schlichte schnaps, but stamped 'Made in Germany'.
- A claim in an advertisement for a wine from Baden, Merdinger Bühl, that it knocks spots off even the great Burgundies and 'can be proud of its provenance'.
- A reference to home base Heidelberg in a full-page advertisement for the Lamy 'twin pen'.
- The conspicuous presence of the Italian tricolour's red, white and green in an advertisement for the Alfa 164.
- A two-page spread titled, in English, 'Jaguar for believers' on the page showing the luxury limousine in question and 'Jaguar for sceptics' on the page of explanation for those who remain to be convinced of the car's merits. This German-language text focuses attention on the fact that the new XJ6 delivered 'in feinstem Oxford Englisch' ['in finest Oxford English'] exactly what the company's slogan, 'Grace, pace and value for money', promised.
- The Pinot Blanc which is advertised a few pages later is not just any Pinot Blanc but the Alsatian Pinot Blanc.

I commented earlier that the edition of *Der Spiegel* in which these advertisements appeared was concerned with Germany as a nation. More specifically, it concentrated above all on post-unification Germany's status. However, the magazine is less preoccupied with answering the question as to whether Germany was now an emergent world power in the conventional sense than with discussing the essential redundancy of the question itself and the significance of this. Noting with interest that both Chancellor Kohl and his main opponent at the time, Oskar Lafontaine, shared the view that a unified Germany was simply a stage in the process leading to a united Europe, *Der Spiegel* conveys the impression of a nation which is led by people for whom, in Kohl's words, there is 'no return to the nation state' and for whom a preoccupation with narrow national interests would be tantamount to an act of betrayal. On the eve of German unification, therefore, the context in which the above country/region-of-origin advertisements appear is essentially a post-national one. In fact, it may be regarded as the archetypal post-national environment. Five years later, in an essay which appeared in *Die Zeit* on 9 June 1995, the man who had been Holland's ambassador to the Federal Republic of Germany in the period leading up to and immediately following unification (1986–93), Jan G. van der Tas (1995), made the point that Germany's neighbours should not just count themselves lucky that Germany had turned its back on the 'obsolete' model of the nation state, but actively follow Germany's example by striving for what he referred to in a then conspicuously novel way as a 'post-national identity', which in the European context means pooling sovereignty. In other words, Van der Tas argues, the Germans had uniquely drawn the right conclusion from the lessons of the twentieth century: a nation, even one that had suffered defeat and division, could become a thoroughly happy, prosperous and respected member of the international community without clinging to conventional notions of national sovereignty and national glory. Indeed, Van der Tas reminds his readers that a discussion paper on European union produced by Germany's Christian Democrats (the CDU party) had defined national sovereignty in an age of mutually dependent nations as an empty shell. So, for Germany, becoming a 'normal' nation state like Britain or France would be a major retrograde step.

Earlier, I cited *Der Spiegel* as the example of a magazine which had recognised the reality of the post-national, global trading environment. As such, *Der Spiegel* hardly seemed to be the most appropriate context for country/region-of-origin advertising, especially as post-unification Germany was beginning to face up to a post-national destiny. For instance, Germany put its massive economic weight behind the implementation of the single European currency. In the first half of 1999, the Federal Republic was exercising presidency of the European Union. On 29 March 1999, *Der Spiegel* covered the EU summit in Berlin, which had on its agenda major reform issues and the nomination of a new president of the European Commission (the Commission found itself in a state of crisis when all the commissioners resigned in response to allegations of corruption). The summit had also taken place against the background of Germany's involvement in a response to the crisis in Kosovo, which was a product of ultra-nationalism. This involvement saw German troops, in the form of the Luftwaffe, in action for the first time since 1945. Do the advertisements in this issue of *Der Spiegel* show any significant move away from the 'country/region-of-origin' strategy? This time there is no advertisement for Yugoslavian wine, and this is no doubt a reflection of the sad sequence of events in the Balkans since 1990. But the following advertisements are to be found:

- One for Rolex watches, in which the cellist Yo-Yo Ma is shown to exercise the same discernment in his choice of a watch as he does in his choice of a cello. The best cellos, we are told, are in his view from Italy. However, the point is also made that 'one of his favourite instruments' comes from Switzerland, and this is the Rolex Datejust. Pierce Brosnan's stated preference is for Omega 'Swiss made since 1848', as readers are told in English. In the case of IWC watches, on the other hand, the words Swiss and town of manufacture Schaffhausen are two of the features we can make out on the face of one of its up-market (DM 28,500) chronographs.
- Wine from Rheinhessen is recommended as 'the wine-growers' wine'.
- Johnnie Walker's four types of whisky are described as containing 'The Magic of Scotland', while it is claimed that Glenfiddich proves there is only one way of discovering the Highlands.
- One of the cited attributes of lead crystal glasses made by Nachtmann – 'the crystal company', readers are told in English – is that they are 'Made in Germany', and the same designation of origin is visible on the photograph of a watch by A. Lange &

Söhne, while the slogan for Jacoform shoes is 'Qualität – Made in Germany' (Head, 1992).

- Daimler-Benz and Chrysler may have become DaimlerChrysler following the takeover of the American firm by the German one in 1998, but the Chrysler Stratus Cabrio is described as embodying 'THE SPIRIT OF AMERICA'.
- Rotkäppchen Sekt, an East German sparkling wine which has survived the post-unification exposure to market forces, proudly reminds readers of its provenance in Freyburg a.d. Unstrut.

There are no advertisements that use the 'Made in Europe' or 'Made for Europe' strategy.

In an article which appeared in *The Guardian* on 1 December 1992, just weeks before completion of the Single European Market, the journalist Dan Glaister wrote that advertisers, whom he describes as thriving on prejudice, relied on 'the allure of the foreign [...] to create desire' even though the single market appeared to put that strategy at risk, because: 'It threatens to remove not only barriers, but differences'. He observed that 'as the barriers come down', so foreign languages were flooding into adspeak, and he noted those high-profile country-of-origin campaigns which suggested that 'we fall for German know-how' and 'are real suckers for that good old Gallic charm'. In the latter case, he has in mind, among others, the Nicole and Papa commercials for the Renault Clio, and in the former case, the outstanding example for Glaister is Audi's 'Vorsprung durch Technik' campaign, which had used the company's motto to make the car sound unmistakably German, because, 'in car speak, German equals efficiency, robustness, punctuality, reliability, high-quality engineering': 'Stick a few wheels on any old shoe box, give it a German name, and you've got a winner', Glaister quips (Head, 1992). Significantly, perhaps, the Audi campaign was beginning its remarkably successful life in the mid-1980s, not long after the European Community's Economic and Social Committee had expressed the view that a product's country of origin 'did not fill a genuine consumer need'. Not surprisingly, then, the main recommendation from Glaister's article is that consumers should hang on to their national stereotypes, because 'advertisers need them'. If the advertising in *Der Spiegel* is anything to go by, in post-national Germany consumers have done just that.

References

'Measures having equivalent effect: indications of origin', *Proceedings of the Court of Justice of the European Communities*, 10/85, Case 207/83: Commission of the European Communities v United Kingdom of Great Britain and Northern Ireland, 25 April 1985, pp. 1201–13.

'Alle Fäden in der Hand', *Der Spiegel*, 1 October 1990, pp. 18–26.

Glaister, D., 'You're just their type', *The Guardian*, 1 December 1992.

Head, D., 'Advertising Slogans and the 'Made-in' Concept', *International Journal of Advertising*, 7 (1988), pp. 237–52.

Head, D., *'Made in Germany': the Corporate Identity of a Nation*, London: Hodder & Stoughton, 1992.

Ohmae, K., *The Borderless World: Power and Strategy in the Interlinked Economy*, London: Collins, 1990.

Porter, M. E., *The Competitive Advantage of Nations*. London & Basingstoke: Macmillan, 1990.

Van der Tas, J.G., 'Nur nicht 'normal' werden' *Die Zeit*, 9 June 1995.

4   Rhetorical Devices In Television Advertising

P. M. Crompton & R. McAlea
Manchester Metropolitan University

In the classical world rhetoric was one of the seven liberal arts, alongside dialectic, music, grammar, arithmetic, astronomy and geometry (Lausberg, 1996). According to Quintilian, rhetoric, the art of the *rhetor* or orator, was defined as *bene dicendi scientia,* or knowledge of how to speak to a good purpose (cited in Lausberg, 1996:70–83). For others, rhetoric had a more specific aim; for Cicero, as Heinrich Lausberg affirms, 'the purpose of an oration or discourse has as its aim to convince and persuade the listener'.

The type of oration was important in classical eyes. Thus an oration may be *judicial, deliberative* or *epideictic;* that is accusing or defending; exhorting or dissuading, and praising or blaming (Burton, 1996–8). It may appeal to reason (*logos*), to emotion (*pathos*) or to character (*ethos*). The rhetorical text was also divided into distinct parts, each with its own function, beginning with the introduction or *exordium,* the statement of facts or *narratio,* through several named stages until the conclusion or *peroratio.* Each part had an appropriate appeal, deploying logos, pathos or ethos accordingly.

The listener or audience was of special importance in the deployment of rhetoric. For the Greeks, *kairos* meant 'generative timeliness' or occasion. For the Roman rhetorician, *decorum* or appropriateness of discourse to the circumstances was what was required: 'to fit one's words not only to the subject matter, but to the audience in a given place at a given time' (Burton, 1996–8).

Each aspect of the rhetorical discourse might be best served by a set or group of rhetorical tropes, and much scholarly effort, from classical times through the Renaissance and into modern times, has been devoted to grouping the linguistic tropes or figures in appropriate categories.[1]

The rhetorical trope or figure was and is simply one aspect of the whole field of rhetoric. Even the simple tropes, of which some are familiar and in everyday use, constitute a tiny proportion of the devices that can be used to defend, to exhort and to praise. Terms such as metaphor, simile, ellipsis, hyperbole, oxymoron, onomatopoeia will probably be familiar to most.[2] Less familiar to some will be the several hundred rather more esoteric terms listed in the various texts and web pages now available.[3] This is not to say that the devices they describe are not deployed in modern texts, but that their classification in rhetorical terms is probably less familiar than it would be to a medieval or classical author, although there has been a revival of rhetorical studies in literary scholarship and in other fields of research.

It might be argued that searching for rhetorical tropes in the language and imagery of the television advertisement is rather like the Molière character who discovers that all his life he has been speaking in prose: that, in other words, these devices are now so well embedded in the language of persuasion and indeed in everyday language that no classical origin need be sought nor identified. This is both true and false.

It is true, in that those who use language and images to persuade may indeed be ignorant of a classical precedent; but it is false in that rhetoric is but a means of classifying those alterations of syntax, grammar and meaning which are deployed to persuade. There may or may not be gifted classical students of rhetoric at work in the advertising industry; but it does most certainly employ gifted creators of word and image. The contention of this paper is that the techniques of persuasion can be analysed according to the classifications of rhetoric which have been extant for two and a half millennia; that the classifications of rhetoric provide a powerful analytical tool; and furthermore, that many such devices can be found in Spanish and English television advertising. As Pedro Barras García (1997: 2) asserts in his article 'La Lengua y la Publicidad':

> Persuasion and making attractive are the objectives of Rhetoric: to make attractive and to persuade are also the aims of the advertising message. Consequently it should not surprise us that the resources used in advertising should frequently rest upon the discoveries of Rhetoric, the efficiency of which is tried and tested.

A total of 108 television advertisements have been analysed, from Spanish and British television. This is not then an exhaustive survey; even allowing for repetitions, it probably accounts for no more than a fraction of the daily output of television advertising in both countries. Nor is it proposed to identify the maximum number of rhetorical tropes in a large number of advertisements; such a study is beyond the scope of a paper of this length, and must await a more appropriate format. Our proposal is to examine closely a small number of advertisements, and show how the rhetorical devices are deployed.

There is a compelling reason for concentrating on two examples. A simple analysis or identification of rhetorical devices would not serve to bring out their full force. For in advertising a combination of visual and audio imagery serves to create a most powerful message. What stands out in the adverts we have looked at is the complex interplay between text and image, so that a secondary rhetoric is created, both visual and auditory. Not the least exciting field of study in the aesthetics of contemporary advertising is the rapid evolution of this complex interplay between visual and audio, and in all cases the underlying rhetoric on which both depend.

Of course there are, aesthetically speaking, 'bad' advertisements as well as 'good' ones, just as there is 'good' and 'bad' poetry. Not all adverts deploy the subtleties of expression and image available to the creative mind; but the examples chosen contain sufficient examples of rhetorical devices, both textual and visual, to support the contention that rhetoric may serve as a useful tool in the analysis of television advertising.

In our multimedia age, television advertising represents one of the most complex of all presentations. Some or all of the following may be present. First the sound: there could be a voice-over, usually one, sometimes a dialogue of two or more people: on-screen actors may speak, either to each other, or enter into dialogue with the unseen voice-over. The characters may be human beings, or cartoons, animations, puppets, speaking in human voices; the voice-over might even be in a foreign language. There may well be music, incidental or central to the advertising theme. The music may have lyrics, which themselves may constitute the principal theme of the advert. There could well be sound effects, not necessarily the sounds associated with the particular product. There are also the visual effects: the images may be 'real life', cartoon, computer animation, or a combination of all three: there may be one or more images simultaneously on screen, either with split-screen techniques, superimpositions, reflections. There may well be a written text, either flat 'on screen', or embedded in the visual imagery, say on the product presented to the screen or within the visual narrative. Sound effects may be presented visually in comic-book style; and the advertisement may be in colour or black and white, or a combination of both.

A multiplicity of messages are being transmitted simultaneously; what is clear is that a complex communicative discourse takes place, much of it simultaneously and on a number of levels, in the space of perhaps twenty or thirty seconds. Finally, the complex whole has to bear repetition; the audience will probably see the advertisement several times, and it will hopefully still intrigue after a number of showings: in other words, it must be sufficiently complex to require several viewings in order to be fully decoded.

We shall now analyse in some detail two advertisements, one each from British and Spanish commercial television.

Advert 1: Rice Krispies

The advert is in the form of plasticene puppets (*à la* Wallace and Gromit), representing the familiar characters of Snap, Crackle and Pop developed by the Kellogg's Company over a number of years, and familiar to British TV audiences. The advert is in the form of an address to camera by one of the characters, subsequently off camera, then back at the end, inviting an inspection of the Rice Krispies 'factory'. The premise of the advertisement is that the sounds made by the cereal indicate the 'full to bursting-point' vitamin content.

Kellogg's Rice Krispies

1st cartoon character to camera/voiceover
Why do Kellogg's Rice Krispies go snap, crackle and pop?
Let's find out.
Listen to those vitamins!

2nd cartoon character
Hear that iron!

3rd cartoon character
This is where the rice goes...*aaaah!*

1st cartoon character
Kellogg's Rice Krispies!
Sounds like they're much more than Snap,

2nd cartoon character
Crackle and

3rd cartoon character
Pop. ugh. . .

First, there is here a case of *anthypophora,* that is, asking a rhetorical question and posing the answer as if in dialogue: 'Why? Let's find out'. Then there are two examples of *synaesthesia,* which is the description of a sense in terms of another one: 'Listen to those vitamins! Hear that iron!' The visual narrative shows fantastical machinery making mechanical noises, and so there is real noise being emitted: we are of course meant to associate the factory noises with actual vitamins and minerals. The two statements are similar in meaning and syntax, and constitute a third device, an *isocolon.* The third character starts to tell us about rice: 'This is where the rice goes..' but at that point falls into the machinery before he/she can finish. An unfinished statement constitutes yet another device: *aposiopesis.* The main character concludes by stating 'Sounds like they're much more than Snap,..' etc. This is an example of an *ellipsis,* where part of the sentence is omitted but easily understood by the audience in the context. (It sounds like).

Finally, 'Sounds like they're much more than Snap, Crackle and Pop' is a *paradox,* two contradictory ideas in one statement, since 'Snap, Crackle and Pop' are *onomatopoeias,* and thus sounds. Which is resolved by the fact that 'Snap, Crackle and Pop' can be interpreted as a *synecdoche,* part for the whole or whole for the part; 'Snap, Crackle and Pop' stands for Rice Krispies. But since in the context they are also the sounds, then we have *amphibologia,* a structure with two possible interpretations. And just as an afterthought, the characters themselves are examples of *prosopopeia,* where the sounds of the cereal assume human (or at least cartoon) attributes.

So, in one short advertisement of thirty seconds duration, we have ten examples of rhetorical devices. Our contention is that these devices are not simply used as decoration or embellishment, but are deployed as an integral part of the persuasive process. The first device, anthypophora, is a device designed to carry one's audience along with the orator: a question is posed in such a manner that the audience is prepared to go along with the narrator to find out the answer. The audience in this case being twofold: the primary audience of the child watching the advert, the secondary audience of the parent who will buy the product. Older viewers of this British television advert may also have recognised the voice of the actor providing the voice-over: the TV personality John Noakes, who was formerly a presenter of a well-known children's programme, probably when most parents were themselves children, and still a household name. The two audiences are skilfully crafted together by this ingenious piece of casting.

The synaesthesia of 'listen to those vitamins! Hear that iron!' is also a skilful use of this device, given the primary audience of children: it explains by imagery the notion of vitamins and trace elements, surely a complex notion to get across to children, and providing the secondary audience with a ready-made catch phrase for their own persuasive efforts.

The aposiopesis is purely for fun: both audiences are more than aware that the third name of the characters/sound of the cereal is 'Pop'. The unfinished statement as the character falls into the machinery is a simple slapstick comic effect. It is also the third character who falls into the machinery: the Holy Trinity of threes so embedded in fairy tales and folk tradition, in humour and religion alike, with here the third slightly smaller character being the loveable chaotic element.

The ellipsis gives a familiar tone to the final utterances, inviting complicity of the primary audience, and at the same time engaging the secondary one. For as the ellipsis invites complicity, the statement also appeals to the reason or *logos* of the secondary audience: if the cereals sound like they're much more than 'Snap, Crackle and Pop', then perhaps they are. The paradox, onomatopoeia and amphibologia here work together, creating an intriguing message on a different level for parents: 'Snap, Crackle and Pop' may convince your children to eat the cereal: *you* know that it is more than a simple gimmick to get them to eat, for the food is full of vitamins. By ostensibly aiming the advert at children, and thus inducing a 'willing suspension of disbelief', in Maurice Bowra's famous phrase, a very subtle, very adult message is put across. The devices of rhetoric in this language of persuasion are in our view most skilfully deployed.

Advert 2: Vileda

We would now like to discuss an advertisement from Spanish television, Antena 2, transmitted in 1993. It is a somewhat more complex advertisement than the Rice Krispies commercial, and provides an example of both textual and visual rhetoric. It contains a number of textual rhetorical devices, and has integrated these with the images on a number of levels. The advert is for Vileda mops and lasts twenty seconds.

The text is as follows:

Vileda *Floor mop*

Voice-over, male

A veces los que más queremos	At times those we most love
Son los que más ensucian.	Are those who dirty (things) most.
Por eso Vileda presenta	For this reason Vileda presents
Su nueva fregona suave.	Its new, gentle mop.
Más ligera y manejable.	More manageable and lighter.
Así limpia y seca más.	So it cleans and dries more.
Ayúdate con Vileda	Help yourself with Vileda
Y también la bayeta suave de Vileda.	And also the gentle Vileda cloth.

(Subsequent references will be to the Spanish text only, since some of the rhetorical devices do not translate effectively into English.)

The advertisement opens with three shots of a group of day-old chicks on a white tiled floor, crossing the screen from left to right, in increasing close-up, with the faint sound of cheeping. On the second close-up the voice-over begins 'A veces los que más queremos...' The third shot closes in on the messy footprints, coinciding with the text 'que más ensucian'. Next there is a close-up of the mop itself, angled bottom left to top right, at quite a suggestive angle. As we hear 'Por eso Vileda presenta', the head of the mop is attached, with the satisfying click which is an audio quote from every militaristic action film; it is the sound of an automatic weapon being primed.

Then the cover is removed from the mop, ready for action, and as a visual metaphor for 'suave, más ligera y manejable', the head of the mop waves about in slight slow motion as if the hair of a woman were being shaken. This is also what McQuarrie and Mick call 'resonance', the visual images reflecting and interpreting the textual ones. On 'manejable', there is the sound of cheeping again, and an ascending electronic arpeggio. The mop goes into action, this time from right to left in reverse direction to that of the chicks, with a subdued sound of jet engines or a high-speed car. The action echoes the line 'así limpia', and as the phrase 'y seca más' is uttered, we see a close-up from below of the mop being squeezed out and the sound effects of echoing drops of water, as if the water were falling from a long distance; an auditory metaphor; the dirt has been sent a long way away. The water too is improbably clean, suggesting perhaps that our loved ones do not really make that much dirt. There is a final shot of the mop, still going right to left, as it chases the last chick away. There is another arpeggio, as well as the powerful jet sound; but this time the arpeggio is of the echoing drips we heard a moment earlier; another auditory metaphor to suggest that the mop will clean up the very last drop, as the arpeggio goes off the scale. But of course our attention is on the scurrying chick, hygienically shunted off the stage; a powerful symbol once more; for if the chicks were metaphors for children, this last chick becomes a symbol again, for now the mop even takes care of the children. And of course we have met this individual chick before. In a previous incarnation it was Dopey, in *Snow White and the Seven Dwarfs;* it was the little mushroom in *Fantasia* that couldn't quite join the circle of dancing mushrooms; in Spielberg's *Close Encounters* it was the last smaller extraterrestial light that almost didn't make it back to the mother ship; and in the Rice Krispies advert, it is the third character who falls into the machinery. It is a powerful visual allusion, holding our attention as the message gets to work.

Interesting too is the angle of the mop. For while the mop is following the chick, the person wielding the mop is off screen, drawing the chick towards him or her; all is forgiven, the errant young creature is being drawn back into the fold. The advert ends with a visual text and a still shot of the Vileda mop and cloth.

More than with the Rice Krispies advert, there is a complex interplay between the textual rhetoric and the visual rhetoric of the images. The rhetorical devices of the text begin in the very first line, 'Los que más queremos. ... .son los que más ensucian'. In this pairing of phrases there is an anaphora, the same structure repeated: 'los que más,...los que más'. But in the Spanish there is a change of subject encoded in the verbs: 'queremos' means 'we love', and 'ensucian', 'they make dirty', since the Spanish verb system is inflected, the subject of the verb shows in the endings *–emos* (we), *-ian* (they). This has a curious effect: for although the structures appear virtually parallel, the morpho-syntax is different: *los que* in the first part of the structure is the object of the verb *querer,* to love: in the second half of the structure *los que* is the subject of the verb *ensuciar,* to dirty or make dirty.

There is also within this anaphora a double *antithesis*, with the second terms of each antithesis suppressed. Consider: the opposite of *querer* (to love) is not *ensuciar,* (to make dirty) but rather *odiar* (to hate); similarly, the opposite of *ensuciar* is not *querer,* but *limpiar* (to clean). This double antithesis by having a member of each pair unstated creates a most powerful association: *querer* (to love) equals *limpiar* (to clean); likewise *ensuciar* (to dirty) equals *odiar* (to hate). This double antithesis or suppressed correlation, immediately creates a paradox, so beloved of advertisers: create a problem, then offer a solution.

The potential of the utterance is also heightened by the double visual *metaphor* associated with the relative pronouns 'los que...los que'. In this case, day-old chicks are the referents. The chicks are what we love; their dirty footprints what is hated. Their appearance ought to constitute essentially bathos, since 'querer' is hardly a term we would use with chickens. But there is a powerful visual syntax that occurs here: the bathos is avoided by the expedient of having the chickens appear first, before the voiceover begins. Thus visually we have a rapid transition from symbol to metaphor, a transition effected by the sequence in which the information is presented, by the clever interaction of audio and visual. For the appearance of the chickens most powerfully suggests the symbolic power of the associations they evoke; innocence, vulnerability, need to be protected, the automatic 'aah' factor that urban Western society seems universally to bestow on cuddly animals, especially young animals. But the moment 'más queremos' is uttered, the symbol becomes a metaphor; through the process of a reverse *catachresis*, which is the use of an inappropriate term for description. The qualities of the chicks stands for the qualities of those we most love; the unspoken referent of the second term of the metaphor is of course very young children.

Next we are told 'Por eso Vileda presenta'; here is the solution, in a structure called *hypotaxis,* linking the following clause in such a way as to show its relationship to the preceding one. This is followed by the product description 'su nueva fregona suave'. 'Suave' is repeated in the same structure in the last intervention, 'la bayeta suave de Vileda', and constitutes an *epistrophe*, albeit rather a weak one, which is the repetition of the same term at the end of a line or phrase. Perhaps it might be more appropriate also to term this a permanent epithet, since each mention of the products of Vileda is accompanied by the same adjective: 'fregona suave', 'bayeta suave'.

The next utterance appears to be a classical rhetorical structure: 'más ligera y manejable, así limpia y seca más'. This inversion of word order in a balanced structure is a *chiasmus,* and also an example of *epanalepsis*, that is repetition of a word (in this case *más*) at the beginning and end of an utterance. There is also a mild *alliteration* 'ligera', 'limpia', and to achieve the chiasmus there has been an ellipsis: either '*Es* más ligera', starting a new utterance, or less likely, '*que es* más ligera', continuing as a relative clause. But how effective is the ellipsis, since it allows what appears to be the symmetry of the chiasmus.

In the penultimate utterance, there is an example of *eponym*; replacing the object with a proper name 'Vileda' instead of 'fregona': since if we follow on to the next line, 'y también la bayeta suave de Vileda' the first mention in this syntactic group of the term 'Vileda' must refer to the mop itself. Even so, the last utterance does not grammatically follow from the previous one: 'Ayúdate con Vileda, y también la bayeta suave de Vileda'. There is either another ellipsis, 'Ayúdate con', or in the context the ellipsis could be 'hay' (there is), or some such impersonal verb, as in 'también hay la bayeta suave de Vileda'. (There is also the gentle Vileda cloth). But the sentence does not finish with a grammatical structure coherent with the first part, and this device is called an *anacoluthon*. So in terms of the use of rhetoric, we have identified some eleven devices in the Vileda advert.

Before we evaluate the rhetorical devices in this advertisement, some attention must be paid to an element not present in the previous one; written text. The text on the screen is presented on three levels. First, bottom right on screen throughout the advert is the brand name Vileda; second, the brand name is shown on the products in the closing shot, both the mop and the cleaning cloth. Third, there is 'product placement', if that is the right description, during the action; the sheath removed from the mop is imprinted with the name Vileda, as is one of the strands of the mop head itself.

In the Vileda advertisement the voice-over narrative and the visual narrative are mutually dependent: without the visual images the narrator would be making rather an illogical claim about the mop. Without the voiceover, the visual narrative could seem to be claiming that mops were useful to clear day-old chicks out of a kitchen. The rhetorical devices in the spoken text and the visual images together create secondary associations that reinforce the principal message. The initial anaphora of 'los que más queremos son los que más ensucian' binds together in its apparently balanced structure three quite disparate notions. First, of course, the idea is planted that even in a perfect, aseptic world (the pristine kitchen floor) dirt can sometimes intrude (the tiny muddy footprints of the chicks). Second, that the things that are loved belong to 'us' (*queremos*) whilst what is hated, the dirt, is 'them' (*ensucian*). Third is the visual detail of the chicks 'invading' the kitchen as they move from left to right across the screen. They shouldn't be there; chicks have no place in the kitchen; and if they have muddy feet, they have come from 'outside'. All this reinforces the double antithesis: we love the chicks, we hate the dirt. The paradox has been established: individual children – the visual metaphor of the chicks – are 'you'; their muddy appendages are 'they'. How can we love children and hate their feet? This paradox is even stronger in the Spanish language since parts of the body are referred to by expressions including the definite article 'the', rarely if ever by the possessive adjectives 'my', 'your' 'her', and so on. The clever use of day-old chicks of course removes responsibility from these creators of chaos: we would suggest that much stronger emotions would have been aroused if, for example, an unlovely teenager had created the mess; the love element would certainly be diminished. The innocence of the image helps preclude any negative emotion from the scene; even in the midst of chaos, we are cushioned against any deeper feelings.

Any stirrings of unease or deeper feelings are soothed by the solution Vileda 'presents'; not just a mop, but a gentle mop. But we are not let entirely off the hook emotionally, since as the mop is assembled there is the menacing click as the mop-head fits into place; and the angle of the mop suggests a more robust attitude: even if we love the chicks, dirt is serious. The claim made for it is held together by the apparent chiasmus of 'más ligera y manejable, así limpia y seca más'. What this nicely balanced phrase puts together is that because the mop is lighter and more manageable, it therefore cleans and dries more. This is simply not a logical claim, yet seems to hold together in the structure bounded by 'más...más'. Curiously the logical fallacy of this phrase seems to be echoed by the internal grammar: *ligera* and *manejable* are both adjectives, whilst in the second half of the phrase *limpia* and *seca* are both verbs. Yet the visual images at this point also echo the break in the logic and the grammatical dissimilarity. For as we hear 'más ligera y manejable', the head of the mop begins to sway in slow motion, mimicking the head of a woman shaking her tresses; the mop is now a light and manageable woman. But as the second half of the phrase is spoken, we see the business end of the mop being squeezed out, and then the sound effects of a powerful engine as the mop chases the chicks across the screen, now right to left. Upright, the mop is a metaphor for the woman or man of the house; inverted, it is the enemy of dirt. The powerful switch of image, if anything, disguises the illogicality of the claim made for the mop. The paradox established in the opening lines has come down on the side of cleanliness. If anything the chiasmus reinforces the visual images, and the chiasmus is itself reinforced by the use of 'más. . .más', repeating the same two terms used to express our love-hate relationship with children-dirt. But lest we think that Vileda offers an over-drastic solution, the mop does not exactly pursue the chicks back across the floor, for once again the image is softened and made less threatening by the fact that the mop is drawing them towards the person doing the cleaning. Finally, any lingering subconscious thoughts about drastic solutions to deal with dirty chicks are assuaged by the repetition of 'suave' (gentle) as a permanent epithet for Vileda mops. All these elements are crammed into twenty seconds of densely packed information. Yet the advert seems effortless, almost guileless, unhurried.

We hope to have shown that classical rhetorical tropes can be of use in analysing both the textual and visual elements in television advertising. It is not our claim that rhetoric provides a unique solution, but rather that it can serve as a powerful tool in the analysis of the complex interplay of elements that constitute this medium. This we contend is not an exaggerated claim, since as we stated at the outset, rhetoric as a classical discipline in the liberal arts was precisely that branch of human knowledge deployed to persuade, to defend, to praise. Advertising is surely the medium *par excellence* that attempts this.

Notes

1   A very small sample of these works would include: Aristotle, *The Art of Rhetoric*. Trans.by John Henry Freese, Loeb Classical Library, 1982. Quintilian, *Institutio Oratoria*, Trans. H.E. Butler, Loeb Classical Library, 1920–2; George Puttenham, *The Arte of English Poesie*, 1589, Kent State University Press, 1988; Warren Taylor, *Tudor Figures of Rhetoric*, Whitewater, WI: Language Press, 1972; Lee A. Sonnino, *A Handbook to Sixteenth Century Rhetoric*, London: Routledge & Kegan Paul, 1968; T. Albaladejo, *Retórica*.

Madrid, 1989; E.P.J. Corbett, *Classic Rhetoric for the Undergraduate Student*, Oxford, 1990; W. Nash, *Rhetoric; the Wit of Persuasion*, Oxford, 1989; B. Vickers, *In Defence of Rhetoric*, Oxford, 1988.

2   All definitions of rhetorical tropes are taken from Gideon O. Burton (1996–8), where the appropriate classical and Renaissance authorities are also cited. Where Burton differs from other authorities, particularly Albadalejo, Corbett, Harris and Nash, these are also quoted. If definitions differ significantly, in the last resort the Oxford English Dictionary has been used, i.e. *The Shorter Oxford English Dictionary*, (2 vols), 3rd ed., Oxford, 1968.

3   In addition to those sources cited above, an increasing number of Internet sources on rhetoric have proved useful. These include:

Robert Harris, 'A Handbook of Rhetorical Devices', South California College, August 1997: http://www.uky.edu/ArtsSciences/Classics/rejext.htm; and of course the author already cited, Gideon O. Burton, 'Silva Rhetorica'(1996–8), at: http://www.humanities.byu.edu/rhetoric/silva.htm.

References

Barras García, P., 'La Lengua y la Publicidad', *Español Actual*, 33 (Junio 1977).

Burton, G.O., 'Branches of Oratory', *Silva Rhetorica* (1996–8), at: http://www.humanities.byu.edu/rhetoric/silva.htm.

Lausberg, H., *Handbuch der Literarischen Rhetorik. Eine Grundlegung der Litteraturwissenschaft*, Munchen: Max Hueber Verlag, 1960. Taken from the Spanish edition, translated by J. Pérez Riesco, *Manual de retórica literaria: fundamentos de una ciencia de la literatura*, Madrid: Gredos, 1966, pp. 70–83.

5 Voices with or without Faces

Address and Reader Participation in Recent French Magazine Advertising

Béatrice Damamme-Gilbert
University of Birmingham

Until the 1970s or even the early 1980s French advertising might have been described as lagging behind its British counterpart in terms of sophistication and inventiveness. In spite of, or perhaps because of Roland Barthes's pioneering work on the semiotics of the image and popular myths (1957 and 1964), the French intellectual class and French policy makers had for generations been contemptuous of mass culture, perceived as a threat to the preservation of 'high' culture (Rigby, 1991). However, the situation has changed in the last fifteen years or so, partly because of young people's interest in the media and advertising, particularly, as shown, for example, by the popularity of television programmes devoted to it, partly because some intellectuals, such as the well-known philosopher Bernard-Henri Lévy,'BHL', have themselves been mindful of their media profile and partly because the public's increasing standard of education and growing awareness of advertising discourse have meant that advertising messages have started to incorporate a whole range of inventive devices (Sorlin, 1992). This trend shows signs of evolving very fast. Nicolas Riou in his study of advertising and the postmodern society (1999) describes how the public's growing familiarity with the media is making brands fundamentally rethink the way they are marketing themselves.

In the light of these changes, my purpose will be to examine a number of French magazine adverts from the 1990s, assessing how the messages address the receivers and thereby construct for them a position which could be seen as a form of identity. In particular, I would like to consider how voices, coming to us through the language of advertising messages, and combining or contrasting with a visual mode of address, usually a face, elicit an active response from us, and offer an interaction, a participation, which is much more involving than the hard sell or heavily didactic messages of the 1950s and 1960s (Sorlin, 1992), which usually required a passive response from the receiver.

Address will be understood as referring to the way messages challenge us, as readers of the message and as consumers, to produce a response as part of a process of communication. All messages, whether linguistic or not, presuppose the existence of a sender. Three layers can usually be identified in the case of advertising: the company or organisation marketing a product or themselves, the advertising agency that devises the message and the voice whose text is relayed by the message, including the fictional voice of the man or woman represented in the ad. I shall try and examine what linguistic and visual forms are used to challenge and hence construct an image and a position (even a voice) for the receiver who is the reader of the message. Address has been comprehensively studied. Greg Myers, for example, in his discussion of 'Pronouns and Address' (1994), acknowledges his debt to Williamson (1978), Goffman (1979), Winship (1987) and others in this area. This work, together with Benveniste's influential writings on 'énonciation', particularly deictics and tenses (1966), will constitute the theoretical background for my analysis.

This study will focus on (1) adverts displaying a deliberately confusing system of address where humour and the desire to entertain (sometimes through intertextuality) play a crucial part and (2) adverts showing evidence of a self-aware, reflexive discourse where the receiver is positioned as capable of deconstructing the subtleties of advertising discourse – or at the very least as an active, not a passive recipient.

All the advertisements analysed here appeared in *Télérama*, a television, radio and cinema magazine with a wide appeal, addressing both genders equally, but aimed in particular at the fairly affluent and well-educated market. The ads selected all promote either a product comprising some form of modern technology (hi-fi, car, camera) or a technologically advanced service (the TGV train).

The first advertisement to be considered will serve to remind us of the potential for ambiguity provided by the use of pronouns when combined with a face. This is a 1994 advert for a Harman/Kardon hi-fi system. Visually, the ad features a young woman, sitting on the floor of what appears to be a sitting room (she sits at the foot of an out-of-focus green sofa). Her posture is relaxed and informal, her arms are crossed, cradling her raised knee. At the very centre of the page, her right leg is bent in a sharp angle and its shape is emphasised by the tight-fitting leggings down to the bare feet on the floor. In close proximity to her stands the hi-fi, its height matching that of the raised knee and giving the impression that the young woman is also cradling it. She stares at the camera but the face, in the optical centre of the page (Vestergaard & Schrøder, 1985), is turned sideways, allowing the light coming from the right to give a slight sparkle to her eyes. She smiles contentedly and perhaps invitingly. The face staring at us with bright eyes is an exceptionally powerful device for making the viewer feel involved, directly addressed. Blanche Grunig (1990) contrasts the face looking straight at the camera – which she compares to a head of state's address to the nation: we know he is addressing millions but we are invited to feel personally concerned – with the sideways, dreamy glance which allows us, so to speak, to go through the glass and identify with the reflective stance, to adopt as ours the character's inner discourse. The sideways glance is also a seductive address, less directly challenging but more suggestive, offering a possible sexual invitation. Here this is reinforced by the physical posture which conveys a moment of relaxed informality. We are situated in very close contact with the character (as she is in close contact with the hi-fi). The bare feet and the tightly fitting leggings serve as markers of potential intimacy – echoed possibly by the slogan in small letters 'la passion du son' (the passion of sound). We may enter the picture and identify with her comfortable posture and be 'her' but we may also – presumably this applies mainly to male viewers – be lured by the promise of her inviting bright eyes, which feed our desire. The shadowy background and the subdued colours allowing the focus to rest only on her and the hi-fi add to the suggestion that she may be the embodiment of our dream – in close association with the hi-fi of course.

Linguistically the advert is made up of several short texts which address us in different ways and do not form, superficially, a cohesive whole (headline, body-copy, name and brand, signature and slogan, offer of catalogue) but which all contribute, lexically at least to the totality of the message. Only one, the headline, is constructed with personal pronouns. 'Elle et moi, on est fait pour s'entendre...', which translates as: She and I (but also, theoretically, 'it and I') we are made for each other; literally: to get on with each other/or: to hear each other (because of the polysemy of 's'entendre') or even: be heard.

The text which follows is written from the non-personal position of utterance of the company, in the third person and with no direct exhortation to the reader:

> Belle et intelligente, la chaîne Festival hérite d'une conception audiophile issue de la technologie HARMAN/KARDON la plus sophistiquée, associée à une facilité d'emploi et à une élégance totalement dédiées à une seule cause: la qualité d'écoute.

> (Beautiful and intelligent, the Festival hi-fi system benefits from an audiophile design, the product of the most advanced HARMAN/KARDON technology, allied with ease of use and an elegance totally devoted to a single outcome: listening quality.)

The text provides an important linguistic clue with the feminine noun 'la chaîne' (the hi-fi system) which generates another referent for the pronoun 'elle': It; and of course 'entendre' (to hear) belongs to the same lexical field as 'hi-fi', hence the pun.

If we forget the picture for a moment and consider the headline, the most obvious interpretation would be that this is about a relationship between two people, such is the force of the cliché 'made for each other'. The 'she' would then have to be the young woman portrayed in the picture, which would leave the 'I' position for the voice speaking through the headline. The expected identification would then be that 'I', the receiver of the message, can become the voice who speaks the headline, and enjoy a relationship with the young woman – which would match exactly the seductive visual message. This meaning is reinforced by the text which uses a number of lexical items obviously attributable to a woman: 'belle, intelligente', 'élégance' (beautiful, intelligent – in the feminine – elegance).

The second interpretation is that the young woman is adopting the subject position and referring to her enjoyment of the hi-fi, whether they are made for each other, or they can 'hear each other well' or even 'be heard well' (the reflexive can have a passive meaning in French). The pun is easily grasped thanks to two clues: the polysemy of 'entendre' and the use of 'faire': to make, which fits the idea of a relationship encapsulated in the cliché and reminds us that audio technology had to me 'made', manufactured. As addressee we would then be invited to identify with her inner discourse: we have already bought the hi-fi and can describe our satisfaction.

It could be argued that what we have here is a classic case of what Judith Williamson (1978: 29–31) called, after T.S. Eliot, the objective correlative – the desirable qualities of the woman are transferred to the object, and vice-versa. Only here, the contrast between the hard geometrical and metallic features of the hi-fi and the softness of the young woman's image adds an extra twist, open to interpretation: is she to be equated with a piece of equipment, or is she expected to relate to it and transform it? More is achieved even, due to the multiple reference attributable to the pronouns, in conjunction with the picture. A plurality of identification for the receiving position is made possible: she can be our dream, we can both purchase her and purchase the dream when we purchase the hi-fi, but we can also be her and enter the dream bubble. Moreover, the reader is given the pleasure of enjoying a pun, invited and empowered to play with the different layers of the message. Perhaps this is what the seductive glance is partly about: not so much beckoning with a promise of intimacy, but rather inviting us to make the most of the ludic interaction inscribed in the message.

My second advertisement, which shows the bottom half of a woman sitting on a bench on a railway platform, might as easily as the previous one be discussed under the rubric of gender issues. We notice, for instance, that the motif of the female leg – diagonally displayed from left to right – is repeated here. This advert for the well-known TGV service of SNCF, the French National Rail Company dates from 1995. It is specifically marketing their Paris-Bordeaux service and is aimed openly at first-class users. The unspoken text is that the service can compete favourably with an internal flight, indeed it is *better*; the text below the strapline invokes preference: 'à nous de vous faire préférer le train' (up to us to make you prefer the train). The headline, to which I shall come back, announces: 'All businessmen will tell you, in first class, they have more room to spread out – literally unfold – their papers (dossiers)'. The failure to specify what the comparison 'more room' is with might imply: more room than in second class; but this is surely too obvious, so the more subtle implication must be: more room than in a competing service, a French domestic flight perhaps. This sharply competitive stance is disguised behind a rhetoric which claims, very effectively, that the service offers a perfect match between requirements and fulfilment, satisfying our desires so entirely that first class travel becomes simply a way of travelling, no longer a luxury but a way of life.

Rather than being stared at by an inviting pair of eyes we are confronted here – and this is the main visual impact – with only a pair of very long and feminine legs, complete with high heel shoes, whose owner's face and upper body have been left out of the picture frame. The visual code is explicit, we are invited to adopt a voyeuristic, not to say fetishistic stance. Other visual associations come to mind, such as adverts for tights or high heel shoes; and the light and gleaming black-and-white background of what looks like a very modern but empty train station invites questions as well as possibly conjuring up associations with station scenes in black-and-white films. Why is she alone? Although we cannot judge her facial expression, the sitting position suggests waiting, not only for a train but for someone, perhaps a lover. The vast emptiness surrounding her calls up thoughts of other human figures. A rendezvous or a parting, fraught with emotional intensity, are all potential associations here if the addressee interprets the black-and-white photography as an allusion to black-and-white films, known to enjoy a popular appeal amongst the cultured French public: films such as *'Jules et Jim'*, or even *'Casablanca'* where the station (rarely as empty as here, admittedly) features as a place where relationships are put to the test. We are therefore indirectly invited to read the moment as emotionally or sexually (because of the erotic motif of the legs) significant. However, the relationship between the headline and the picture provides a problem which, superficially, may not be as easily resolved as in our previous example. Using 'vous' ('you' second person singular formal style or second person plural), the voice of the text seemingly addresses the potential user(s) of the service from a position of accepted knowledge 'Tous les hommes d'affaires vous le diront' (All businessmen will tell you).

But we need to consider how the picture, and particularly the interaction between picture and text, modifies the process of address and therefore our reading of this ad.

First of all, in spite of my comment about the 'you' referring to the consumer, the presence of a human figure opens up other possibilities: the 'you' may be addressed to her – she is probably, after all, one of the passengers – or perhaps, she is addressing us from within the picture; but this is more problematic because there is no face to anchor the communicative exchange. We are, in fact, deprived here of an obvious identification.

Secondly, there is no 'I', the voice is not locatable. The headline is a statement which relays indirectly someone's words. But the view expressed is representing accepted knowledge, common to a whole social group, 'businessmen', metonymically signalled by one of their typical attributes, 'dossier' – papers or files – which appears in the headline.

This is where the picture intervenes again in our search for a coherent meaning, by posing a number of questions. The figure is clearly not a businessman but she could be a businesswoman and the papers are obviously present on her lap. Perhaps we are being teased or challenged over our gender stereotyping: this woman should perhaps be identified and therefore addressed as someone belonging to the class of businessmen. Or perhaps she is waiting for her male business partner or colleague, who may or may not be her lover. Politically-aware readers might see an allusion to the French debate centred on the feminisation of job titles ('homme d'affaires' is certainly a more widely recognised phrase than 'femme d'affaires') and may also feel tempted to question the real meaning of 'affaires', although the sexual connotation is far less established in French that it is in the English 'affair' (the obvious French equivalent of 'affair' being 'liaison' or 'aventure').

The next polysemic element, designed to generate humour, is the phrase 'déplier leurs dossiers' (spread out – literally 'unfold' their papers) which, juxtaposed to the picture, readily suggests the French expression 'déplier leurs jambes' (uncross their legs). Together with 'dossier' which can mean the 'back of a seat' (and therefore suggests: open out the seat) they invite the astute reader to imagine a scenario (or scenarios) for a sexual encounter.

46

What is striking is that the advert carefully avoids offering one consistent meaning and therefore disrupts the process of identification. It teases us and challenges us to match image and words and explore potential further meanings offered by connotations and puns. Although it targets men, it certainly doesn't exclude women – even if some may feel offended. It is possible that the play with gender switching may be echoed in the unresolved contradiction between the vast space of this empty station and the necessarily cramped even if vastly improved, space on any train. Questioning difference may well be one of the underlying themes here. The text below the picture switches modes of address, it avoids personal pronouns until the very last sentence 'soyez les bienvenus' (Welcome!) which enters into dialogue with the company slogan 'à nous de vous faire préférer le train' (up to us to make you prefer the train). The interplay of first and second person pronouns is noticeable here. It foregrounds an explicitly close relationship of exchange between addresser and addressee, stressing the complete devotion of the company to service, but also explicitly stating its aim to *persuade* us that the train is better. This makes the marketing process totally transparent and, in a way, defuses the rather teasing, or even confusing, message delivered by the headline and the picture. However, it could be argued that teasing us, entertaining us, is a different way of engaging our attention and therefore winning us over. Humour and the pleasure derived from appreciating puns seem, here, the main intended effects of the rather ambiguously playful system of meanings image and text combine to produce. This necessarily calls into question the precise identity constructed for the addressee. The sexual dimension may be offensive but, in the context of less than puritanical French advertising, it is at least *intended* to amuse, and the puns would suggest that we are invited to stand back from the advert, not take it seriously (since it is not taking itself seriously), which, in turn, might imply that we have the capacity to understand the allusion to other visual texts such as sexist adverts or black-and-white films. The slogan which discloses unashamedly its own purpose, credits the addressee with the ability and sophistication to accept the advertising process whilst being entertained by wordplay and challenged to play intertextual games.

I would now like to consider briefly adverts which seem to take further this open acknowledgement that advertising is a discourse of which both addresser and addressees are fully aware and in which they are happily participating. In other words, I am interested here in the self-referential elements which seem to be, in the context of French advertising at least, one of the hallmarks of the new generation of adverts.

One type of self-referentiality is illustrated by a 1997 advert for the Ford Ka, a car which is small and relatively cheap but has immense style. It uses a very simple device: a double spread in a magazine allows a large, virtually full-size (in the original of the magazine that is) reproduction of a steering wheel, telling the reader openly, in the headline, 'Tournez ce magazine un demi-tour à gauche, un demi-tour à droite pour apprécier la direction assistée de la Ka' (turn your magazine half-way to the left, half-way to the right to appreciate the Ka's power steering), the French 'assistée' suggests 'aided, assisted steering'. Although no one will believe in the efficacy of what is proposed as a way of gauging the car's performance, what is interesting here is the directness with which the headline unself-consciously addresses us as readers of the magazine, as well as potential buyers and drivers of the car. Admittedly, the rest of the body-copy returns to a very conventional addressing stance, creating a fictional addressee who has already bought a Ka and is, of course, delighted with it. But for a moment, the dialogue addresser/addressee seems to circumvent the artificial communicative construction of most adverts and briefly offers something closer to a direct, 'see-and-touch' form of advertising. It may not be irrelevant that the life-size picture of the wheel actually allows the reader to discern some individual features of the dashboard. More importantly, it proposes a new mode of interaction, other than linguistic or visual – one which involves the recipient physically. It belongs firmly to our new world of virtual and interactive museums, video games and interactive TV, where physical manipulation and keyboard or joystick skills are emerging alongside linguistic and visual modes of communication. Perhaps this device could also be seen as akin to the technique of distributing a sample of perfume, a sachet of shampoo or washing powder. Here, however, our potential consumer is not a glamorous woman or a housewife but rather a young man who owns a Play Station with car-like controls, who might appreciate the very modern-looking design of the Ka.

My next example of self-referentiality, a 1994 advert for the Nissan Terrano II, superficially offers a classic case of the objective correlative strategy: the product appears against an idyllic mountain backdrop. Friends or members of a family, in a variety of poses are presenting weather-beaten but happy and fulfilled smiling faces to the camera. However, once we have moved beyond the first level of reading, which is mainly visual, the caption below the picture offers an interesting way of anchoring us, the readers of this magazine, into the fictional representation. 'C'est bien nous, épuisés mais ravis par la marche, devant notre Terrano II etc.' (Yes, that's us, worn out but thrilled by our walk, in front of our Terrano II etc.). The first person plural pronoun – when not representing the company itself speaking to us – usually addresses us from inside the fictional representation, from, for example, a group featured in the picture. Here, however, it becomes clear that the group portrayed are not addressing us directly, they are in fact looking at themselves, looking presumably at a photo of themselves, after the event, sharing their memories of the hike – perhaps with other friends. In passing, they are sharing these memories with us – we are positioned as the privileged witnesses of a happy moment recorded on film. So, far from being asked to somehow enter the picture as if we had taken part in the hike or own a Terrano, we are in effect being asked to enter a fictional construction on a second level, closer to the advertising process itself, the world of photos, visual constructions framing a very special moment in a camera lens.

The effect is twofold; on one hand, the virtues of the product are less blatantly displayed than in traditional adverts; the product becomes part of a rich family heritage, worthy of featuring inside a photo album, of being preserved as an image and a topic of conversation and therefore of playing a part in the construction of a social identity; on the other hand, the reader of the advert is credited with a more sophisticated outlook. The visual metalanguage of advertising reveals itself. Our identity as addressees is not only grounded in our awareness of social and cultural values expressed through discourse but also in our ability to interpret our lives visually.

It should be noted that this interpretation does not apply to the text below the caption which switches to a more traditional mode of address: the voice-over commenting on the emotional and technical benefits of the car, and opting for the 'you' as the addressee who either has been or is about to be seduced into purchasing. 'Il y a des heures où la vie prend tout son sens. Le Terrano II vous accompagne dans ces moment-là.' (There are times when life becomes fully meaningful. The Terrano II is with you at those times).

The final advert to be considered takes the self-referential technique to the point of making the addressee aware of her powers as someone capable of constructing a world visually and thereby inviting her participation in the creative process. It is perhaps not surprising that it is an ad for a camera, the Canon EOS 500S. We have another double spread, this time presenting us with a visual puzzle. We see what looks like an open-top wedding car driving towards us. The presumed groom is just about visible on the far right of the picture, at the wheel. The bride however is engaged in exchanging suggestive sideways glances with a dashing motorcyclist riding alongside the wedding car, also riding towards us. The headline is made up of three questions without answer: 'Ex?' (standing, of course, for ex-husband or partner). 'Coup de foudre?' which means 'love at first sight' and finally 'félicitations?' (congratulations). It takes a little time to understand who is saying this and to whom. The text below the picture gives us the clue by addressing us, the consumer and reader of the magazine, telling us to write our own story with the Canon camera featured in the bottom-hand corner. The three questions are three different scenarios which could be applied to the same visual construction captured on film. One should add that there is another possible ambiguity: 'écrivez votre propre histoire' (write your own story). This could be the story you are writing – or the story of your life. This last connotation is invited by the context of the wedding as a momentous event.

So, not only are we made fully aware of the visual text we are invited to read when we look at an advert, but we are ordered explicitly (notice the imperative form) to select the meaning for ourselves and perhaps to create our own photo-novel. The effect clearly here is to encourage the active participation of the receiver. Of course this works particularly well because we are dealing with a camera advert, which thus succeeds in extending the appeal of the product not only to record stills but to offer the potential for creating a visual narrative, not dissimilar to a filmic text. It is striking, however, that we are not addressed from within the picture, not asked to identify with any of the characters – we are addressed as if we could ourselves be the addressor, the creator of the message. The slight delay experienced by the receiver in understanding the headline will only add to the satisfaction of being given control of the exact meaning of the ad.

I have examined some devices and strategies which, although relatively recent in French magazine advertising, are becoming more widespread strategies which certainly offer a much broader range of positions to the receivers of advertising messages than was the case fifteen or twenty years ago. Interaction and active participation, which are often fun-inducing, are the key features. Offering several interpretations simultaneously, playing with pronouns and their reference, disrupting the identification of voices and faces, inserting puns and other features of humour are all crucial in the attempt to avoid a passive receiving mode – something which is a strong marketing imperative for any advertiser looking for an efficient return on his investment. There is now also an acknowledgement that French receivers are more sophisticated. They can be positioned as adept readers of visual messages; so that making the message self-referential and often intertextual will not be at all counter-productive. This is neatly demonstrated by a 1997 advert for a soft-top Golf Cabriolet Coast car, displayed on a sandy beach below the headline: 'demain, j'enlève le haut' (tomorrow, I'm removing the top). It re-uses a well-known earlier campaign for the advertising company 'Avenir', which had featured three successive posters where a young female facing us in her bikini was announcing that 'on the 2nd September, she was going to remove the top' then, topless: 'on the 4th she would remove the bottom'. The third poster showed her naked, but from the back, whilst the caption read: 'the advertiser who keeps his promises'. Whilst intertextual reading is not compulsory here, its potential for entertaining the receiver is enormous.

Stimulating the reader's visual and cultural memory as well as ludic ability will mean that she or he feels both intelligent and in charge, more actively involved in the production of multi-faceted meanings. Although this strategy will be seen as a ploy to flatter the consumer, better to lure him or her, it must also be understood as reflecting one of the most important features of postmodern culture.

References

Barthes, R., 'Rhétorique de l'image', *Communications*, 4 (1964), pp. 40–51. Available in translation in *Image – Music – Text*, London: Fontana, 1977.

Barthes, R., *Mythologies*, Paris: Seuil, 1957.

Benveniste, E., *Problèmes de linguistique générale*, Paris : Gallimard, 1966, particularly part V, 'l'homme dans la langue', chapters 18–23.

Goffman, E., *Gender Advertisements*, London: Macmillan, 1979.

Grunig, B., *Les Mots de la publicité: l'architecture du slogan*, Paris: Presses du CNRS, 1990.

Jouve, M., *Communication et Publicité*, Paris: Bréal, 1994.

Myers, G., *Words in Ads*, London: Edward Arnold, 1994.

Rigby, B., *Popular Culture in Modern France: a Study of Cultural Discourse*, London: Routledge, 1991.

Riou, N., *Pub fiction: société postmoderne et nouvelles tendances publicitaires*, Paris: Editions d'Organisation, 1999.

Sorlin, P., 'Is Advertising a Characteristic Element of Contemporary French Culture' in Chapman, R. & Hewitt, N. (eds.) *Popular Culture and Mass Communication in Twentieth-Century France*, Lampeter: Edwin Mellen Press, 1992, pp. 101–13.

Vestergaard, T. & Schrøder, K., *The Language of Advertising*, Oxford: Blackwell, 1985.

Williamson, J., *Decoding Advertisements: Ideology and Meaning in Advertising*, London: Marion Boyars, 1978.

Winship, J., *Inside Women's Magazines*, London: Pandora, 1987.

6   What makes a Promotional Brochure Persuasive?

A Contrastive Analysis of Writer Self-reference in a Corpus of French and English Promotional Brochures

Yvonne McLaren
Heriot-Watt University

Introduction

This study takes as its starting point the assumption that corporate brochures are designed primarily to persuade: providing information is an important secondary function, but the main objective of promotional materials of all kinds, advertising included – and indeed the corporate brochure can be seen to be a form of advertising – is to persuade the reader to become a customer of the company. This objective influences the way in which writers design their texts, including the choices they make with regard to the structural characteristics of texts and their lower-level linguistic and pragmatic phenomena. The persuasiveness of the corporate brochure therefore derives from the collective functioning of a range of features, including, for example, positive self-evaluation by the writer (the company responsible for producing the brochure), transitivity patterns which project the company as a dynamic and influential actor, and the use of categorical assertions which create a feeling of greatcertainty about the quality of service provided by the company ((McLaren, 1999).

The forms and patterns of writer self-reference in corporate brochures also serve the promotional/persuasive function. In this study writer self-reference will be examined in a corpus of English and French corporate brochures, with a view, firstly, to establishing how writer self-reference is typically effected by writers of this genre in English and French, and, secondly, to identifying any differences which may exist between the strategies adopted in each language. As will be shown, there are clear trends of writer self-reference forms in the corpus and, furthermore, these trends differ between the French and English brochures. The contention is that the forms selected in each set of brochures and the patterns of their use are motivated by strategic concerns and consequently that, along the parameter of writer self-reference at least, persuasiveness is achieved in different ways by their French and English writers.

Following examination of the conventions of writer self-reference, our attention will turn briefly to another genre, namely that of printed advertisement. It will be shown that there are noticeable differences between the two genres in relation to the degrees of personality and directness which characterise writer self-reference. This is true in both languages but is especially evident in the case of French. It will be argued that the contrasts stem from genre-related conventions of writer-reader interaction: differences in the way in which writer-reader interaction is conducted are associated with the use of different forms (here writer self-reference forms) on the surface of the text and are evidence of the different persuasive strategies in operation.

Previous studies

A number of important studies have compared features of written French and English (e.g. Chuquet & Paillard, 1987; Guillemin-Flescher, 1981; Vinay & Darbelnet, 1958 & 1995). However, these have tended to be general studies, concerned chiefly with issues related to translation between the two languages, particularly at the level of the sentence and below. Although they cover personal reference, pointing to the fact that in English the preference is for the use of personal and animate forms, while in French there tends to be a preference for the impersonal and/or the inanimate, their conclusions tell us nothing about how personal reference may be strategically motivated, and, since they discuss only individual sentences or utterances, they are not able to identify patterns in the use of such forms over the course of a text. It will be from this perspective that writer self-reference will be studied here.

Such concerns have been addressed in other studies, however, which focus primarily on English. Myers (1989), for example, in his investigation of the pragmatics of politeness in a corpus of scientific articles, finds that forms of personal reference may be manipulated for strategic purposes. For example, "One way of making a criticism . . .is for the writers to use pronouns that include themselves in the criticism. Besides the we that means the writers, there is a we that means the discipline as a whole" (1989: 7).

Thompson & Thetela (1995: 103–27), for example, examine related issues in their analysis of writer-reader interaction in a corpus of newspaper and magazine advertisements collected between 1991 and 1993 and examine such issues as writer and reader roles, power relations, naming strategies and degrees of visibility of interaction. With regard to the identity of the writer, firstly, they note that what is important is not who actually wrote the text, but who is represented as the 'writer-in-the-text'. In the advertisements they analyse, this tends to be the company as a whole, although variations on this are possible, such as 'Our engineers'. Secondly, they note that, 'The presence or absence of a writer-in-the-text, his/her identity, and the way in which s/he is referred to will clearly have an effect on the way the interaction is managed' (pp. 110–1). In advertisements, 'The most common ways in which the writers refer to themselves are as we and by using the company name', and in many cases the phenomenon of referential switch where 'the writer switches between the two forms of labelling within the advertisement' (p. 117) can be found, sometimes even within the same sentence. Such a switch 'confirms that the third-person forms, the company names, are to be taken as having first-person reference' (p. 118). This phenomenon is illustrated in example 1 (p. 117):

1. And that's exactly why *Lufthansa* will never abandon its uncompromising commitment to the very highest standards of quality and service.
That's why, for instance, we are constantly expanding our network.

Furthermore, Thompson & Thetela find that there are a variety of explicit and implicit forms of writer self-reference which can be placed along a continuum, with the result that 'the speaker/writer may appear in the text, for personal or interactional purposes, with greater or lesser degrees of visibility' (p. 109). Writers may choose not to appear on the surface of the text at all. If they do opt to appear explicitly , various means of self-reference may be adopted: the company name, the first person plural pronoun 'we', or a mixture of both. Such choices are not, however, made arbitrarily: 'If only third-person forms referring to the organisation are used with no switch to first-person forms, this suggests that the writer is writing on behalf of an impersonal and thus authoritative organisation which is inherently third-person and exists above and beyond any individuals in it' (p. 118). Although it is noted that this may be appropriate for some advertisers, Thompson & Thetela find that the majority 'exploit referential switch to carry out the two functions of projecting overt interaction and thus intimacy with the reader, and yet ensuring that the reader cannot lose sight of the identity of the addresser' (p. 118).

As will be shown in the analysis which follows, writer self-reference is also an important tool in the corporate brochure. It is used by writers as a means of negotiating their relationship with readers and is thus an important part of their strategy of persuasion.

The Corpus

The data analysed for the purpose of this study are a corpus of 25 French- and English-language corporate brochures, amounting to just over 52,000 words in total, which were published in the mid-1990s and collected between November 1996 and April 1997. Twelve of these brochures are written in French and were produced by private-sector companies in France, while thirteen are written in English and were produced by private-sector companies in the UK. All of them were produced for external purposes (as opposed to in-house documentation, for example) and are designed to promote the company itself and the products and services it provides, and ultimately to persuade the reader to become a customer. The corpus therefore consists of what Hartmann (1980: 38) terms 'texts created independently in similar situations in their native-language cultures' , selected on the basis of similarity of purpose (persuasion), text producer (private-sector company) and text receiver (potential customers).

Examples are given below from brochures for the following firms:
- Tilbury Douglas Construction, a construction engineering firm;
- Ethicon, a manufacturer of surgical equipment;
- Marie Brizard, a drinks company;
- Laboratoires Dolisos, a firm which specialises in homeopathic medicines.

Through a series of analyses and confirmatory checks, the examples cited have been established as representative of the typical trends in the English and French brochures, and are used here for the purpose of illustration only.

Patterns of Writer Self-reference in the Corporate Brochure

The specific objectives of the analysis were as follows: firstly, to identify whether writer self-reference is typically realised by relatively personal or relatively impersonal means (e.g. first person versus third person forms) in the French and English brochures; secondly, to establish which forms are most frequently used (i.e. is one form – e.g. the subject pronoun 'we' – particularly favoured?); thirdly, to show whether, over the course of any given text, a pattern emerges in the choice and use of writer self-reference forms; and finally, on the basis of this, to seek out any systematic contrasts between the strategies of the French and English writers.

Conventions of the English Brochures

Prior to the analysis itself a cline was established showing the range of forms available for potential use by English writers for the purpose of self-reference. These forms vary in terms of the degree of 'directness' or 'personalisation' involved, as can be seen in Figure 1.

This cline is a representation of the type of continuum mentioned by Thompson & Thetela (1995) since, as we move from left to right, the forms used to realise writer self-reference become relatively less explicit. The most direct or 'determinate' (Stewart, 1995) form available for the purpose of writer self-reference in English is clearly the first person singular pronoun 'I', since 'I' signals most clearly the identity of the speaker or writer. This is followed by the use of exclusive 'we' (where 'we' excludes the reader), and then by the use of inclusive 'we' (where 'we' includes the reader and approximates to 'you and I'). It should be noted, however, that distinguishing between cases of 'we' used exclusively and cases of 'we' used inclusively involves judgements that can never be made with total certainty.that distinctions between cases of *we* used exclusively and cases of *we* used inclusively can never be made with total certainty.

The pronouns mentioned so far and indeed all of those included in Figure 1 are

personal	›		›			impersonal
direct	›		›			indirect
--------I--------------I--------------I--------------I--------------I--------------I--------------I						
1	2	3	4	5	6	7
	excl.	incl.	generic		3rd pers. forms	impersonal structures
I (sing.)	We	We	you	one		
[subject	›	object	›		possessive] [animate/ inanimate]	[animate/ inanimate]

Figure 1. Writer Self-Reference: Forms Available for Potential Use in the English Language System

subject pronouns. However, object pronouns and possessive adjectives may also be used. Indeed, opting for one of these may be a deliberate strategy: the use of the subject pronoun *we*, for instance, is more direct and involves a stronger degree of visible reference to the speaker or writer than the object pronoun *us*, or the possessive adjective *our*, which, although also first person plural forms, appear to be more subtle indicators of the presence of the writer in the text. This is reflected in examples 2 and 3 from the Tilbury Douglas Construction (TDC) brochure:

> 2. With an enviable level of repeat business and serving many of today's major organisations, our impressive track record extends to Commercial and Retail developments, Educational, Health, Leisure, Residential and Industrial buildings, …
> 3. We have been established in the Middle East for 20 years and have an impressive track record of important projects …

In both of these examples a very similar statement is made about the company and its track record. However, reference to TDC is effected by different means in each case: whereas the possessive adjective *our* is used in example 2, in example 3 the subject pronoun *we* is used. This would seem to create a difference of effect: *our* makes a less visible reference to the writer than the subject pronoun *we*: where the possessive adjective is used, the attention of the reader is drawn to the noun *track record* rather than the adjective *our*, whereas in example 3 there is no option but to focus on *we* as a personal representation of the company. It is for this reason that the subject – object – possessive distinction has been included in Figure 1.

As we move along the cline from left to right we come to forms which are rather less personal and which are increasingly implicit means of writer self-reference:

- the generic pronoun 'you';
- the indefinite pronoun 'one';
- third person forms which are variable in terms of the degree of animacy or inanimacy they incorporate;
- and finally impersonal structures in which the writer does not feature explicitly at all but may be inferred as being present, e.g. agentless passive constructions such as 'Over £4 million is invested annually in internal and external training courses'. (This example is taken from another brochure in the corpus, produced by Christian Salvesen Distribution).

These are the forms available for potential use. However, only some are actually used in the English brochures under examination here: these are the pronoun 'we' (used exclusively and inclusively) and its associated forms, various third person forms and impersonal structures. It should be noted, however, that inclusive 'we' and impersonal structures are rare. The infrequency of occurrence of the latter may be the result of a desire on the part of the writer constantly to focus the reader's attention on the company by explicit means.

The fundamental choice for the writers, it would seem, is whether to opt for first person forms such as 'we', 'us', or 'our', or some third person form. The range of third person forms used by the English text producers consists of the company name (e.g. Tilbury Douglas Construction) and various co-referring expressions, i.e. 'different linguistic items [used] to refer to the same concept' (Hatim & Mason, 1990: 240): nouns such as 'the company', the third person pronoun 'it', or the possessive adjective 'its'.

Although instances of all of these categories can be found in the brochures, the favoured third person naming devices of the English writers are the company name, the pronoun 'it' and the possessive adjective 'its'. Indeed, the company name tends to recur throughout texts and brochures, often in conjunction with 'it' and 'its'. Nominal co-reference (the company, the firm, the group, etc) is much less common.

Overall, however, the writers of the English-language brochures tend not to use these forms in a sustained manner. They seem to prefer to use the first person pronoun 'we' and its related forms, especially the possessive adjective 'our' + noun. This preference is reflected in examples 4 and 5, which are taken from the Ethicon brochure.

4. *Our* commitment to quality is demonstrated in a number of ways.
5. Recognising *our* responsibilities to customers, employees and the community, *we* strive to utilise the best practices in all *our* products and processes.

First person forms are not, however, used in all instances of writer self-reference within a given text. Instead, they are used in conjunction with the company name, with the result that a mixture of forms is found. Nonetheless, the choice of which form to use at a given moment in the text is not a random one: the writers tend to alternate between forms and adopt Thompson & Thetela's (1995) strategy of referential switch, where the writer starts off by using the company name and then switches to first person forms. Consider examples 6-7:

6. *Tilbury Douglas Construction* is today one of the largest construction companies in the United Kingdom, and *we* are proud to have made a major contribution to the built environment of this country.
7. The customer is key to all *ETHICON* activities. This commitment to customer care drives *our* extensive research programme and the on-going continuous improvement of products and production methods.

If we refer back to the cline in Figure 1, we can see that, by adopting a strategy of referential switch, writers move along the cline from right to left (position 6 to position 2), in the direction of increasing determinacy, personalisation or directness. We find, therefore, that, whereas at the outset more impersonal forms tend to be used, a switch takes place to more personal forms. Possible reasons for this will be suggested below.

It is not the case, however, that third person forms are never used again: indeed they may well be used at any subsequent stage. The fluctuation between first person and third person forms of writer self-reference in example 8 is typical of the English brochures.

8. Tilbury Douglas Construction is today one of the largest construction companies in the United Kingdom, and we are proud to have made a major contribution to the built environment of this country.

Over the years *the company* has gained extensive experience in most of the sectors of construction, on projects both large and small.

With an enviable level of repeat business and serving many of today's major organisations, *our* impressive track record extends to Commercial and Retail developments, Educational, Health, Leisure, Residential and Industrial buildings, Water, Sewerage and Highway schemes as well as the full range of Civic and Local Authority developments.

In this example we have a progression from the company name [Tilbury Douglas Construction] to the subject pronoun 'we', to the co-referring expression 'the company', and finally back to a first person plural form, namely the possessive adjective 'our' [our impressive track record]. This is a very typical pattern in the English brochures. As we shall see in the next section, however , it is not at all common in the French brochures: choices made by the French writers – and indeed their overall strategy – would appear to differ significantly from those of the English writers.

Conventions of the French Brochures

Prior to the analysis of writer self-reference in the French brochures a cline similar to that given in Figure 1 above was established for the French language and is given below in Figure 2.

From Figure 2 it is clear that the most direct way for a writer to refer to him/herself in French is to use the first person singular pronoun 'je': where 'je' is used, there can be no doubt as to the identity of the speaker or writer. This is followed by 'nous', the first person plural pronoun, used exclusively and inclusively. Regardless of the way in which 'nous' is used, it is much less specific as a means of reference than 'je': exactly who constitutes 'nous' is in both cases unclear. This point is also made by Stewart (1995).

When using any of these forms, French writers, like their English counterparts, have the choice of whether to opt for the subject or object pronouns, or the possessive

personal	›		›		impersonal
direct	›		›		indirect
--------I--------------I--------------I--------------I--------------I--------------I					
1	2	3	4	5	6
	excl.	incl.		3rd pers. forms	impersonal structures
Je (sing.)	nous	nous	on		
[subject	›	object	›possessive][animate/ inanimate]	[animate/ inanimate]	

Figure 2. Writer Self-Reference: Forms Available for Potential Use in the French Language System

adjective. As we noted above, this can be a strategic choice, since the possessive adjective would appear to be less direct and therefore a less obtrusive marker of the writer's presence in the text than the object pronoun, which would seem in turn to be less direct and less obtrusive than the subject pronoun.

If writers in French do not wish to use any of the first person forms, they may choose to opt for relatively less personal referring expressions:

- the pronoun 'on', which, according to Judge & Healey (1985: 57), 'is regarded as the nonspecific form of the third person singular pronoun subject' and which Stewart (1995) noted to be the least determinate of all the personal pronouns;
- third person forms, ranging from clearly animate to clearly inanimate entities and covering a variety of differing degrees of animacy and inanimacy in between;
- or impersonal structures in which reference to the writer is merely implied, e.g. agentless passives, nominalisations, etc.

Actual instances can be found in the French brochures of all the forms indicated in Figure 2, except for the first person singular pronoun 'je' and its associated forms. However, it should be noted that inclusive 'nous' and the pronoun 'on' (which is probably too informal for this genre) are used only rarely. This is also true of impersonal structures which were noted above to be rare in the English brochures too.

What is perhaps most striking in the French brochures is that first person plural forms, which are very common in the English brochures, are much less favoured. Indeed, a quantitative analysis showed that, whereas in the English brochures 39.28% of all instances of writer self-reference are in the first person, in the case of the French brochures this figure is only 11.4%. Furthermore, many of the French brochures contain no reference using 'nous', 'notre', 'nos', etc. at all, whereas it is virtually impossible to find such an absence of first person plural forms in the English brochures.

It is the use of third person forms which tends, therefore, to characterise the French brochures. There are several types of third person forms, broadly corresponding to the categories identified in the English brochures, i.e. the company name and various forms of nominal co-reference (*l'entreprise, la société, le groupe,* etc.) and pronominal co-reference: the third person singular pronouns 'il' and 'elle', the object pronouns 'le', 'la', and 'lui', and the associated possessive adjectives 'son', 'sa' and 'ses'.

Judging by the examples found in the corpus, the following examples are typical instances of writer self-reference in French corporate brochures:

9. *Le Groupe MARIE BRIZARD* a toujours disposé de *son* propre réseau de distribution…

(The *MARIE BRIZARD Group* has always had *its* own distribution network…)

10. La politique de formation et les perspectives de carrière offertes par *Dolisos* sont les facteurs clefs de *son* dynamisme.

(The training policy and career prospects offered by *Dolisos* are the key factors behind *its* dynamism.)

As reflected in these examples, the company name used in conjunction with third person singular pronouns and possessive adjectives is a particularly popular strategy. This is significant for two reasons.

Firstly, as we noted above in relation to the English brochures, the company name tends to be used repeatedly with relatively little recourse to forms of nominal co-reference, although there are variations on the company name. In the brochure for Laboratoires Dolisos we find both 'Laboratoires Dolisos', and simply 'Dolisos' (example 8) while in the brochure for Marie Brizard, 'le Groupe Marie Brizard' (as in example 9) alternates with 'Marie Brizard'.

The fact that nominal co-reference is rare in the French brochures under examination here is significant since it suggests that, in this respect, the corporate brochure in French is very different from other genres in French, notably newspaper articles in which nominal co-reference is a conventional feature, as Hatim & Mason (1990: 97), for example, have noted.

Secondly, and perhaps more importantly, it would have been perfectly feasible for the French writers to employ more personal forms, as in the following non-occurring examples:

11. *Nous* avons toujours disposé de *notre* propre réseau de distribution...

(*We* have always had *our* own distribution network...)

12. La politique de formation et les perspectives de carrière que *nous* offrons sont les facteurs clefs de *notre* dynamisme.

(The training policy and career prospects *we* offer are the key factors behind *our* dynamism.)

Although there are some instances of first person forms in some French brochures in the corpus, it is far more usual for third person forms to be used throughout. The standard progression is therefore from company name to third singular person pronouns and/or possessive adjectives, followed by alternation in the text between these two sets of forms, similar to the movement we noted in the English brochures between company name and first person plural forms. These findings suggest that the French writers choose to employ rather less personal forms of writer self-reference than their English counterparts. Why should this be so? Let us now turn our attention to possible reasons for this tendency.

Accounting for the Differences between the French and English Brochures

There are clearly significant differences between the two sets of brochures in the patterns of writer self-reference. As has been shown, the trend in the English brochures is for the writers to begin by referring to themselves by means of the company name and then to switch to first person forms (especially the possessive adjective 'our' + noun), and thereafter to alternate between first and third person forms. In the French brochures, on the other hand, the writers again begin the text with the company name as the preferred means of writer self-reference but then switch only to other third person forms, with the result that the French brochures, at least where this feature is concerned, are rather more impersonal than the English brochures.

This conclusion partly confirms the view of numerous contrastive linguists working with French and English (e.g. Chuquet & Paillard, 1987) that English tends to be more personal than French. However, as we have seen, the situation in the corporate brochures examined here is more complex than that implied by this simple dichotomy, since patterns emerge over the course of each text, suggesting that we need to look at whole texts rather than isolated sentences.

How can the differences between the English and French brochures be explained? As was noted above, Iit is a contention of this study that the patterns of use of certain linguistic and pragmatic features, including writer self-reference, are components of the text strategy writers adopt as a means of achieving their primary purpose, in this case persuasion. Part of this strategy involves the creation of a relationship, conducive to successful persuasion, between the writer-in-the-text and the reader-in-the-text. The choice of forms used on the surface of the text, including those which realise writer self-reference, can therefore be seen to be motivated by a specific purpose: to shape the writer-reader relationship. The switch to first person forms by the English writers, for example, may serve to reduce the distance which inevitably exists between writer and reader at the outset of a text and to help a more 'friendly' relationship develop as the text unfolds. In the view of the English writers this may be a prerequisite for successful persuasion. Such an approach suggests that they are prepared actively to influence the writer-reader relationship for their own strategic purposes. The fact that the French writers, on the other hand, opt systematically for less personal third person forms, suggests that they are less prepared to attempt to manipulate their relationship with the reader in this way and that they are content to maintain a greater degree of impersonality and distance between writer and reader. This does not mean, of course, that they are not engaged in persuasion like their English counterparts. Clearly they are. However, the means they adopt to achieve their objective would appear to be more subtle, suggesting that they perceive the strategy of the English writers as too overt and therefore as inappropriate. Different norms of politeness would seem to be in evidence in the English and French texts.

Comparing Patterns of Writer Self-reference in Corporate Brochures and Commercial Consumer Advertisements

In this section the typical patterns of writer self-reference in French and English corporate brochures are compared with those in commercial consumer advertisements, in an attempt to ascertain whether the patterns of usage are similar across the two genres.

As noted above, Thompson & Thetela (1995) find that there is a tendency in English advertisements towards the use of first person plural pronouns and possessive adjectives and 'referential switch'. In this respect, the differences between English-language corporate brochures and advertisements are not great. However, once referential switch has been effected within an advertisement (and this tends to occur very near the beginning), the use of personal forms ('we', etc.) is sustained to a far greater extent than is the case in the corporate brochure.

In the case of French corporate brochures and advertisements, on the other hand, a much greater difference exists with regard to the forms of writer self-reference typically used. First person plural forms, for example, are very frequently used in French advertisements. This is illustrated in example 13 which is taken from an advertisement for the watchmaker Baume and Mercier (Pons-Ridler, 1994: 96):

13. En 160 ans, *nous* n'avons jamais perdu une seconde.

(In 160 years, *we* have never lost a second.)

The pronoun 'on' is also frequently used for writer self-reference, as in example 14. (In this example and example 14 below 'on' has been translated as 'we'. The direct equivalent, 'one', is much more formal than 'on' and would therefore be inappropriate.

14. Chez Osram, *on* ne pense qu'à ça.

(At Osram, that's all *we* think about.)
(Adam and Bonhomme 1997: 47)

Furthermore, both 'nous' and 'on' may be used inclusively. In example 15, which is taken from an advertisement for EDF, the French national electricity company, we have the use of an imperative which calls for a response from both writer and reader, while in example 16, the pronoun 'on' would seem to refer jointly to the writer (the bank, CCF) and the target audience:

15. L'électricité, *profitons*-en, n'en *abusons* pas. EDF.

(Electricity, *let's take advantage* of it, *let's not exploit* it.)
(Pons-Ridler 1994: 98)

16. *On* a tout de même le droit d'oublier d'appeler sa banque pendant la journée, non? CCF.

(*We all* have the right to forget to call our bank during the day, don't *we*? CCF.)
(Pons-Ridler 1994: 101)

Clearly, in terms of writer self-reference, the producers of French advertisements use a wider range of terms, including the most direct and personal options, than the writers of French-language corporate brochures. Indeed, in the genre of the advertisement, the strategies of French and English writers, at least in terms of writer self-reference, are very similar.

Why should this be the case? It would seem from the evidence adduced above that the writers of French advertisements do not view the use of first person forms as excessively direct or personal. Indeed, from the degree of frequency with which they are used, it would seem, on the contrary, that they are considered highly appropriate and even a vital means of helping create a friendly, helpful, trusting relationship between producer and receiver of the advertisement, which is itself an essential part of persuasion. In corporate brochures, on the other hand, sustained use of personal forms would appear to be considered not appropriate: judging by the infrequency of their use, as they would seem to be perceived as unacceptably direct and intrusive. Impersonality, objectivity and distance would appear to be the order of the day in the corporate brochure. These findings suggest that, whereas the norms governing the realisation of writer self-reference are very similar where English-language corporate brochures and advertisements are concerned, this is not the case in corporate brochures and advertisements in French. This may well be due to the differing degrees of writer-reader interaction considered appropriate by the respective text users.

Conclusion

This study has identified the forms typically used for the purpose of writer self-reference by the writers of corporate brochures in French and English, examined the patterns which emerge in the use of these forms over the course of any given text, and subsequently pointed to differences in the text strategies typically adopted by the writers of French and English corporate brochures.

It has also suggested that examining writer-reader interaction may help us explain some of the conventions and systematic differences identified, since the choices writers make would appear to be inextricably linked to the persuasive purpose of the text, the achievement of which depends on the creation of an appropriate writer-reader relationship within the text world. As we have seen, what is 'appropriate' in the corporate brochure varies between the two languages: the relatively more personal forms used by the English writers suggest that a greater degree of 'closeness' or intimacy between writer and reader is sanctioned in the English brochures, as well as a greater degree of control by the writer over the reader, while in the French brochures the use of more impersonal forms suggests that the French writers prefer to maintain a relatively greater degree of distance between themselves and their readers, and a more even distribution of power.

A further contrast was noted between corporate brochures and advertisements with regard to writer self-reference and persuasiveness. In advertisements writer self-reference is effected by relatively more direct and personal forms than is the case in corporate brochures. This is true in both languages, but more especially in French. The writers of French advertisements appear to have few qualms about being intrusive or manipulative. Indeed, it would appear that a high degree of personalisation in advertisements has become such a conventionalised feature of the advertiser's strategy that it is expected and hence is not perceived by either party (writer or reader) as inappropriate. An advertisement which was characterised by impersonality would probably be perceived as 'odd'., and not even as an advertisement at all, with the result that it would fail to fulfil its intended purpose.

The conventions of English and French corporate brochures differ in much the same way: along the parameter of writer self-reference at least, what is perceived to be persuasive by one set of writers does not tally with what is deemed to be persuasive by the other set of writers. Findings such as these have highly significant implications, not least for translators of corporate documentation whose job it is to produce target language texts which are as effective and successful as the source texts from which they are derived.

References

Adam, J-M. & Bonhomme, M., *L'Argumentation publicitaire: rhétorique de l'éloge et de la persuasion,* Paris: Editions Nathan, 1997.

Chuquet, H. & Paillard, M., *Approche linguistique des problèmes de traduction anglais-français,* Gap: Editions Ophrys, 1987.

Guillemin-Flescher, J., *Syntaxe comparée du français et de l'anglais. Problèmes de traduction,* Gap: Editions Ophrys, 1981.

Hartmann, R.R.K., *Contrastive Textology: Comparative Discourse Analysis in Applied Linguistics,* Heidelberg: Julius Groos, 1980.

Hatim, B. & Mason, I., *Discourse and the Translator,* London: Longman, 1990.

Judge, A. & Healey, F.G., *A Reference Grammar of Modern French,* London: Edward Arnold, 1985.

McLaren, Y., *'Text Strategy as an Interactional Feature in the Corporate Brochure: An English-French Contrastive Textology', PhD thesis, Heriot-Watt University, Edinburgh, 1999.*

Myers, G. (1989), "The pragmatics of politeness in scientific articles". *Applied Linguistics,* 10 (1), 1-35.

Pons-Ridler, S., 'Nier pour convaincre', *La Linguistique,* 30:2 (1994), pp. 93–104.

Stewart, M.M., 'Personally speaking… or not? The strategic value of *on* in face-to-face negotiation', *Journal of French Language Studies,* 5:2 (1995), pp. 203–23.

Thompson, G. & Thetela, P., 'The sound of one hand clapping: The management of interaction in written discourse', *Text,* 15:1 (1995), pp. 103–27.

Vinay, J-P. & Darbelnet, J., *Stylistique comparée du français et de l'anglais. Méthode de traduction,* Paris: Editions Didier, 1958.

Vinay, J-P. & Darbelnet, J., *Comparative Stylistics of French and English: A Methodology for Translation,* Sager, C. & Hamel, M.J. (trans. & eds.). Philadelphia: John Benjamins, 1995.

7 This is your Lifestyle
Self-Identity and Coherence in some English and Spanish Advertisements

Robin Warner
University of Sheffield

One of the clearest instances of the increased attention devoted in critical social theory toward the end of the last century to symbolic forms in general and linguistic communication in particular is provided by Jürgen Habermas's theory of communicative action (Habermas, 1984 & 1987). The key importance consistently attributed to language in this influential work is borne out, at a more practical level, in discourse studies, where there is a widely shared perception that the way people make sense of language is inextricably bound up with the way they make sense of life in general. As one practitioner (de Beaugrande, 1980: 30) neatly puts it, 'the question of how people know what is going on in a text is a special case of the question of how people know what is going on in the world at all'. My aim here is to bring a cross-disciplinary approach to further exploration of an initial intuition: that there are important links and parallels between the concept of coherence in discourse pragmatics and that of identity in critical social theory. Just as an individual's notions of personhood are not formed and sustained in isolation, but are interlinked with the beliefs and practices of the collectivity – as Habermas (1990: 200) remarks, with perhaps unaccustomed bluntness, 'no-one can maintain his identity by himself' – so the ways we use language to organise and conduct our lives 'are deeply embedded within the cultural frameworks by which we make sense out of experience' (Schiffrin, 1994: 371). This underlying interconnectedness of life and language, it will be argued, can be exploited for persuasive purposes. Both coherence and identity are very broad and complex topics, and theoretical exposition of them here must, of necessity, remain somewhat cursory. Nevertheless, some basic concepts will be presented before narrowing the focus to rhetorical aspects of discourse coherence as manifested in a sample of advertisements which seem designed to engage, in one way or another, with addressees' notions of self-identity. The majority of the texts analysed are in Spanish but a number of English examples are included to afford some cross-cultural perspective.

Identity and Lifestyle Choices

For the moment, and although some further elucidation will be necessary, we can remain with the circumspect definition of coherence proposed by David Crystal (1994:

70) as 'the underlying functional connectedness of a piece of language'. Identity, on the other hand, is a widely used and, where precision of sense is concerned, often abused term. It would be as well, therefore, to establish the intended scope of its meaning for the purposes of the current analysis. The focus is on individual self-identity rather than identity as group membership, always bearing in mind that it is rarely possible to draw straightforward distinctions between the collective and the personal in this area of human experience. The French sociologist Pierre Bourdieu (1992: 224) observes that while all sense of identity has a 'core of particularity', it is also essentially 'that being-perceived which exists fundamentally by recognition through other people'. A further perspective is provided by the socio-political theorist Anthony Giddens, one of whose expositions of a critical theory of modernity specifically engages the topic of self and society: 'to be a "person" is not just to be a reflexive actor but to have a concept of a person as applied both to the self and others' (Giddens, 1991a: 53). It is Giddens's model of self-identity as a reflexive project, a biographical narrative or life-plan created by choosing among potential story-lines (1991a: 55 & 75) that provides the theoretical framework for the arguments which follow.

A key concept in Giddens's account of identity is that of lifestyle. The notion of lifestyle is, of course, one which is prominent in the domain of consumption and advertising, and it is true that many routine choices in our daily lives involve a conflation of consumer and minor lifestyle decisions. In a recent interview (Finn, 1999), the social anthropologist – or so-called 'style-guru' – Stephen Polhemus, argues that the balance has shifted decisively in favour of a consumer paradigm of personhood: 'increasingly we use consumption to construct our identities, increasingly we are making the objects we buy – the superficial – more meaningful'. This commodified view of personal identity is strikingly echoed by a regular feature, in 1999 and through into 2000, in *The Guide*, the Friday supplement of the *Guardian* newspaper, entitled 'Who are you? What the —— ad says about you', in which a sort of late modern version of scriptural exegesis is performed on a current advertisement to establish the personality, financial status and lifestyle features – in short, the identity – of those at whom it is aimed. Such claims, however, seem jokily exaggerated, more designed to bolster the presuppositions of consumerism and advertising than to acknowledge the genuine range and consequence of the choices which shape each individual's life-definition. It seems more reasonable, then, to accept Giddens's contention (1991a: 81) that the promotional uses of the term constitute a trivialising reduction of a concept – originally developed by the social theorist Max Weber – to do with 'the very core of self-identity, its making and remaking'. In this fuller sense, lifestyles are embraced not only because they fulfil utilitarian needs, 'but because they give material form to a particular narrative of self-identity' (ibid.). Thus not only life's more momentous decisions, but each of the small choices a person makes every day such as to 'what to wear, what to eat, how to conduct himself at work, whom to meet with later in the evening ... are not only about how to act but who to be' (ibid). Admittedly it is in the interests of the producers of advertisements to blur the distinction between consumer choices and those which contribute to personal life-planning at a more serious level, and characterisations of lifestyle which meet Giddens's definition of the term can occasionally be found in advertisements. For instance, one of a series which appeared in the British press during 1999 depicts, under the heading 'Simply Palm', a professional dancer sitting on the ground, bent forward so that the stylish electronic organiser she is holding up occupies the site of her face and head. The text reads:

> Three choreographers I'd like to work with. François' number in Paris.
> Ballet class 10am. Physiotherapy at 4pm. Dinner with Mark 7.30pm.
> The critics' reviews of my performance. Notes on Nureyev's bio.
> Buy another six pairs of leg warmers. Roses to Katya for premiere (hey, who's jealous?)

This advertisement, possibly aimed at the increasing numbers of women for whom work and career constitute the principal life-project arena, presents the product as a genuinely useful *aide-mémoire* for monitoring and coordinating decisions and plans, whether in the personal or professional sphere, of a remit well beyond that of superficial consumer choice.

While such choices are an unavoidable part of our lives since 'we have no choice but to choose' (Giddens 1991a: 81), they are by no means definitive or permanent, given the inherently mobile nature of self-identity, since 'a person's social practices are constantly examined and reformed in the light of incoming information about those very practices' (Giddens,1991b: 39). Lifestyle choices are made in response to changing circumstances and needs, yet they must also sustain 'a certain unity that connects options in a more or less ordered pattern' (Giddens 1991a: 82). Such patterning, moreover, is not simply a matter of autonomous self-monitoring, but is also influenced by the scrutiny and evaluation of others: 'someone who is committed to a given lifestyle would necessarily see various options as "out of character" with it, as would others with whom she was in interaction' (ibid). The construction and maintenance of self-identity, then, is influenced not only by more or less given circumstances such as race and nationality, economic opportunity, visibility of role models, and so on, but also by the individual's concern to maintain an underlying consistency of self-representation through a constant process of modification, a congruity which is monitored both internally and in response to the opinions – expressed or perceived – of others.

Certain similarities may now have become apparent between the selection process just described and the way natural-language communication is achieved via a series of contextually constrained choices of linguistic options. The analogy becomes even more plausible if we bear in mind that the making and sustaining of self-identity itself has an important discursive dimension. According to Habermas (1990: 199), 'unless the subject externalises himself by participating in interpersonal relations through language, he is unable to form that inner centre that is his personal identity'; similarly, Bourdieu (1992: 222–8) stresses the central role of a performative discourse of definition and self-definition in establishing identity, and Giddens himself (1991b: 35) notes that self-monitoring has discursive features in that 'agents are normally able, if asked, to provide discursive interpretations of the nature of, and the reasons for, the behaviour in which they engage'. It seems viable, therefore, to propose the concept of lifestyle coherence as a central element of self-identity, in much the same way that coherence constitutes an essential feature of successful verbal communication. At this point we need to examine the notion of coherence a little more deeply.

Coherence and Argumentation

From a discourse studies perspective, coherence is not an inherent quality of a text, but an interactive achievement, a product of participants' intentions and judgements. However, there are two broad schools of thought as to what sort of properties the term denotes; one, concentrating on the connectedness of relatively small segments of discourse, has tended to look for 'rules governing ways one utterance can be interpreted as an appropriate continuation of the preceding utterance' (Tsui, 1991); the other approach favours a notion of overarching unity and sense-making within a broad sociocultural framework of the sort envisaged by Deborah Tannen (1984: xiv), who posits 'an underlying organising structure making the words and sentences into a unified discourse that has cultural significance for those who create or comprehend it'. Since advertisements are persuasively oriented texts, I propose to concentrate on the specifically rhetorical, or argumentational aspects of coherence. A major advantage of this approach is that it is applicable equally at the macro-level of broad cultural patterns of interpretation and at the micro-level of links between adjacent utterances.

One of the ways we interpret a piece of discourse as making sense is through recognising that the speaker or writer is displaying a consistent orientation in terms of beliefs and goals. The tendentiousness involved here is something we readily recognise in political speeches, sermons, newspaper editorials, promotional brochures, and so on. It is also a central feature, however, of all types of discourse, including spontaneous talk and routine examples of written language. In both overtly rhetorical texts and in everyday pieces of discourse we encounter not just overall consistency, but also, at a more detailed level, particular instances of argumentation constituted by relations between adjacent utterances (Eemeren & Grootendoorst, 1991). Accordingly, the concept of everyday argumentation I am putting forward is based on a binary unit of linked utterances – the building-block, as it were, of more complex structures – defined as providing reasons for, or against, an utterance, with a view to getting someone to think or do something. This model is particularly appropriate for analysing the discursive structure of advertising texts, since their rhetorical effects tend to be achieved precisely by judicious combining and contrasting of highlighted individual utterances and visual motifs. Another point worth bearing in mind, and one whose relevance to the topic of advertising will become evident, is that argumentational coherence is not necessarily the same thing as successful persuasion. On the contrary, our reaction to persuasive texts is often decisively influenced by the awareness that addressors may well be looking to further their own interests, not ours. The intuition that some pieces of discourse are interpreted as coherent precisely because they fail to convince is borne out by the everyday currency of expressions such as 'well, he would say that, wouldn't he'.

In order to bring out the connection between argumentational coherence and the construction of identity it is precisely the element of persuasion that needs to be examined in more depth. The first thing to note is that what addressees are intended to do or think is not necessarily a matter of great consequence. Often, it seems, speakers merely want to demonstrate that they know when it is appropriate to produce reasons, and know what reasons accord with generally shared standards of evaluation. The following example, the opening of a letter to a newspaper advice column from a Mexican teenage girl suffering from shyness, serves to illustrate this point:

Me estoy aislando de todos porque siento que me rechazan.

(I'm becoming isolated from everyone because I feel they don't like me.)
(*El Nacional*, 25 January 1991)

The letter-writer is not claiming her unsociable behaviour is rationally justified; she is merely offering what is assumed to be a more-or-less understandable reason for it. The girl's strategy is to focus on her subjective stance to what is said, mitigating her commitment to its factual truth and so reducing the likelihood of dispute over how the facts are to be interpreted (Schiffrin, 1990: 245). Such expressive self-representations, however, precisely because some measure of exemption can be claimed from the normal testing of reasons against shared standards, can play an important role in the discursive maintenance of self-identity. The delicate nature of the balance between speakers' self-interest and discursively-embodied respect for addressees is even more apparent when the argumentation is of a type more positively aimed at getting someone to do something. Where advertisements in particular are concerned, the strategy, rather than to stress the subjectivity of utterances, is often to emphasise commitment to their factual veracity. The ways such assertions can be made to perform a mitigating function is a feature of advertisements that is worth examining in more detail. Firstly, however, it would be as well to review some basic structural features of argumentational units in general. The following example is taken from a strip cartoon, showing a boy up a tree addressing his evidently less agile companion on the ground beneath:

El toro te ha visto, ¿por qué no subes, idiota?

(The bull's seen you, why don't you climb up here, you idiot?)
(*Condorito de Oro*, 1987)

In superficial terms, the argumentational unit here combines an assertion with a question. In terms of illocutionary force, however, it consists of a warning of imminent danger used as advance justification for a fairly peremptory exhortation. The example well illustrates two characteristic features of everyday argumentation: one is that, rather than offering explanations for given states-of-affairs, speakers tend to provide justifications for performing various types of speech act, such as assertives, directives, commissives and expressives (Eemeren & Grootendorst, 1996); in other words, the model is not 'the reason for that is...', but, instead, 'my reason for saying that is...'. The other is that the argumentational linking of utterances is routinely recognised without the aid of an explicit connector; the boy on the ground, that is, can work out that the first utterance is a pre-justification for the second without any need for an expression equivalent to 'because'. Indeed, it is worth noting that when justifying statements are linked to direct exhortations in advertisements explicit connectors are almost invariably absent. The following examples, which appeared in the national press, in Britain and Spain, toward the end of 1999, are fairly typical in this respect:

Trust us, we know about damp
(*The Independent*, 16 February 2000)

'Estas Navidades regálale una Game Boy. No querrá otra cosa'

(This Christmas give him a Game Boy. It'll be all he wants)
(*El País*, 12 December 1999)

The important point about the inclusion or omission of argumentational connectors is that attention is drawn, in either event, to membership status in the cultural-linguistic community. When connectors are absent, addressees need to be alert to potential argumentational linkages between utterances. This is not simply a matter of knowing the grammar of argumentational discourse; it also involves background knowledge as to the sort of expressed opinion or goal that is not routinely acceptable without provision of reasons. When connectors are present, on the other hand, they serve as an explicit signal of a text's persuasive orientation, so that the issue raised is that of the addressee's competence to evaluate the particular appropriateness and validity of reasons specifically labelled as such.

An instructive example of the effects which can be achieved by the use of explicit supportive connectors is provided by a Rolex advertisement, published in *El País Semanal*, shortly before the 1999 British Open Golf Championship, an event staged, after a long interval, at Carnoustie, a notoriously tricky and demanding course. The text begins by linking the product to famous past winners, 'Carnoustie evoca nombres legendarios: Armour, Cotton, Hogan, Player, Watson y Rolex', and concludes:

Puesto que en este recorrido sólo triunfan los espíritus más fuertes, ¿puede sorprender que Rolex, el reloj elegido por varias generaciones de leyendas del golf, sea el cronometrador oficial?

(Since on this course only the toughest come out winners, is it surprising that Rolex, the watch chosen by generations of golfing legends, is the official timekeeper?)

The effect given here of overt supportive linking (with 'puesto que', 'since') is a ploy typical of a certain class of advertisements in which the reader is probably expected to recognise that the line of reasoning employed does not hold water, and is more of a tongue-in-cheek device for introducing or reiterating other items of information. The real arguments for choosing a Rolex watch, (its cachet as the past and present choice of prestigious figures and knowledgeable administrators) are conveyed *en passant*, as it were, and are thus more likely to be taken on board with no questions asked by readers flatteringly reassured of their competence when it comes to critical evaluation of overtly-claimed reasons.

Remaining with the way argumentational units carry presuppositions as to participant status, but focusing on internal structure rather than external markers, we move to the opening of an advertisement run in 1999 by the Madrid Council Tourist Office.

MADRID
ven en verano
Podrás disfrutar a tus anchas: la mitad de los madrileños está de vacaciones y la otra mitad quiere divertirse

(MADRID
Come in the summer
You'll be able to enjoy yourself at leisure; half the inhabitants of Madrid are away on holiday and the other half are out to have a good time)

This text, superimposed on a panorama of people in a spacious park enjoying various types of outdoor shows and amenities, displays the connector-less sequence, often found in promotional texts, of a directive followed by a justification. One reason for the popularity of this pattern is that each component structurally reinforces the other. The utterance of explicit directives – and it is difficult to imagine a clearer realisation of a command in Spanish than the distinctive second person singular form, 'ven' – is potentially an infringement of socio-discursive good manners, constituting some degree of imposition on the addressee. However, since such an intention is hardly to be expected in an advertisement, the addressee will tend to infer instead that the information about the advantages of a summer visit is being presented as sufficiently valuable as to offset the apparent solecism of communicating it with such urgency. At the same time, the enjoyable state-of-affairs that is promised – the future tense in Spanish often has the illocutionary force of a commissive – encourages interpretation of the initial directive as advisory rather than requestive. The action to be performed, that is, is presented as desirable from the addressee's point of view rather than that of the addressor (Sperber & Wilson, 1995).

Another subtle use of illocutionary mutual reinforcement can be found in an advertisement for anti-hair-loss lotion which appeared in Portugal toward the end of 1999. Fortunately, for translation purposes, there is an English expression of precariousness, 'by a thread' which is directly equivalent to the Portuguese phrase 'por um fio' suggested by the text and the graphics. Next to an image of a small flask of the product suspended by a hair – or a thread – looped around its neck, we read:

A que está presa a vida de um cabelo?
A resposta está no seu cabeleireiro

(What does a hair's life hang by?
Your hairdresser has the answer)

The product is named below the image, with the further information that it is only obtainable in hair salons, in consultation with trained staff. Superficially, neither of the two utterances seems to be a directive, but the illocutionary structure of this advertisement is, in fact, similar to that of the already-considered cartoon with the dangerous bull. The question and the answer supplied can be interpreted, respectively, as a warning of danger and an advisory directive as to how to avoid it.

Directives do sometimes occur in advertisements unaccompanied by justifying reasons, but when this is the case they almost invariably have an unmistakable well-wishing function – a 1999 cigarette advertisement, for example, exhorts 'enjoy yourself every day'. More interestingly, an even more common structure is that of two directives, the second of which functions to mitigate any imposition occasioned by the first. For instance, the advertisement for Habanos cigars run in the British press in the summer of 1999: 'Spend around a tenner. Feel like a million', or, with the directive/justification sequence reversed, a Spanish example from the same period, advertising a brand of mineral water:

Piensa en tus riñones.
Bebe San Vicente

(Think of your kidneys.
Drink San Vicente)

It is especially worth noting that in two of the last four examples the justificatory reasons have to do to not with promised pleasures or useful services, but with avoidance of what is undesirable. With a negativeness of approach which seems geared to heightened perceptions of risk in the late modern age (Giddens 1991b: 124–32), the assurance is that the product will shield the consumer from unwelcome and even harmful eventualities.

When what is self-evidently a well-wishing exhortation is accompanied by explicit reasons, the effect is to create a presupposition that a basic condition for the appropriate utterance of directives is satisfied: that it is in the power of the addressee to perform the action described (Searle, 1979). This device can conveniently be used to introduce further persuasive information about products in the guise of choice-empowerment. Thus, when a text advertising commercial part-time technical courses, (*El Pais, Pasatiempos,* 7 September 1996) closes with a justification in the form of a detailed list of some sixty available courses, preceded by the directive 'Aprende a creer en ti mismo' (Learn to believe in yourself), we readily appreciate that the 'reason for' element here, based on background assumptions that work is an important determinant of life chances, is the confirmation that an extensive range of courses to suit different aptitudes and ambitions is, in fact, available to choose from. What, in the light of contemporary notions of the successfully integrated self, is evidently a well-wishing exhortation, is thus presented as readily achievable, through a neat conflation of the variety of available products and the multiplicity of access to forms of self-realisation. The structure of this decidedly unglossy and straightforwardly functional advertisement is instructive in other ways. In distinctly 'unmodern' contrast to leisure product advertising – which often features sandy beaches as a setting – it highlights the choice between unproductive idleness and productive acquisition of professional qualifications by depicting two youths lying on the beach under the caption:

> Aprende una profesión
> mientras los demás se quedan tumbados
>
> (Learn a profession
> while the rest are lazing around)

and continues in much the same get-a-head-start vein, reminding its readers that summer is a time to either to 'tomar el sol' (sunbathe) or to 'tomar ventajas' (gain an advantage).

The following advertisement, which appeared in rather more upmarket Spanish magazines early in 1999, provides an example of a 'reason against' type of argumentational unit, employed, characteristically, in conjunction with supportive reasoning of the type already considered. The opening text in larger letters accompanies a close-up of a dog's head, superimposed on a sprawled human body and legs, watching televised sport from a comfortable sofa:

> ¿NO PASA TU PERRO DEMASIADO
> TIEMPO VIENDO LA TELEVISION?
> Hoy en día tu perro vive según tu ritmo de vida. Tú ya sabes que a él le encanta estar contigo, hagas lo que hagas, aunque a veces no sea lo mejor para su salud.
> Por eso Friskies ha creado la innovadora gama de alimentación para perros:
> FRISKIES DIGESTION +.
>
> (DOESN'T YOUR DOG SPEND TOO MUCH
> TIME WATCHING TELEVISION?
> These days your dog follows the pace of your life. You know how much he enjoys keeping you company, whatever you're doing, even though it's not always what's best for his health.
> That's why Friskies have created a special new range of nutrition for dogs:
> FRISKIES DIGESTION +.)

Readers will have no difficulty, even in the absence of an explicit supportive marker, in interpreting the initial question as having the force of an accusatory warning, and the two sentences which follow as constituting reasons for uttering it. While a full explanation of the argumentational structure of units comprising 'reasons against' utterances would take up more space than is available here, it will be readily appreciated that the force of the warning is mitigated (and with it the element of implied blame) by presenting the strength of affection between pet and owner as something counter-expected, and therefore of special importance, or 'worthy of the reader's positive regard' as this effect is described in one specialist account of the rhetorical force of concessive connectors (Mann, 1992). The underlying argument might be re-worded as 'you know it's not good for his health, but he loves sitting with you'. The effect is to present the problem not as negligence when it comes to exercising the dog but as the typically late modern one – and again we find the hint of risk – of how to reconcile the competing demands of potentially incompatible lifestyle domains: those of work and leisure, and that of caring, with its obligation to protect the safety of naively vulnerable dependants. It is at this point that an explicit 'reasons for' marker ('por eso', 'that's why') is introduced, signalling an overt piece of argumentation which can only make sense as a claim that the product has been designed with especially sympathetic insight, as it were, with the specific aim of solving the dilemma of a person habitually caught in just such a conflict of roles.

One area where the linkage between argumentational coherence and lifestyle issues is both problematical and particularly marked is that of 'minimalist' texts, brief expressions which tend to appear in advertisements with a strong visual impact. In one type, exemplified by the already-noted advertisement for Habanos cigars, where the text 'Spend around a tenner. Feel like a million' appears above an image of the product, we might note that the first directive functions, in conjunction with the image, as instruction on how to perform the second. There is another type of text, however, common in advertisements for alcohol, fashion garments and fragrances, consisting simply of a brand name or logo accompanying an image. Such laconic texts seem to defy analysis along argumentational lines in that they do not appear to qualify as the minimal argumentational unit of two linked utterances. In any case, such texts often consist of noun phrases, capable, in illocutionary terms, of being interpreted in a number of ways, since 'in principle there is no limit to what a speaker could reasonably expect [a noun phrase utterance] to convey' (Green, 1989). It is possible we are dealing here with the incantatory use of language to establish an identity and differentiate it from others that Bourdieu (1992: 224 & 251) classes as demonstration: 'an act or sort of theatrical deployment through which the group makes itself visible for other groups and for itself'. Guy Cook (1992: 148), on the other hand, regards such utterances as display, with a function something akin to primitive ritual boasting. It is not fortuitous, however, that in most cases the visual element includes a role model, as with the following two examples, which appeared in *Quo* in the Spring of 1999. One advertises ESENCIA LOEWE, a text which, in large letters, together with a picture of a flask of the *eau de toilette* concerned, accompanies an image of the face of a sexually ecstatic woman, viewed so close up over the shoulder of a man she is passionately clinging to as to put the reader virtually in his shoes; the other carries the product name GUESS JEANS, superimposed on an image of an attractive young couple strolling on the beach wearing garments of this brand.

It is worth bearing in mind that we routinely interpret advertisements as urging us, with reasons, to purchase the product, so that simply naming the product is readily interpreted by addressees as an advisory speech act. But it is also – and especially in conjunction with role-models – a means of presenting the product as a lifestyle feature: to acquire it or not it is presented as a decision not so much about how to act – in a consumer sense – as who to be.

Although I have attempted to maintain a certain neutrality, some doubts may have become apparent as to the transparency – and hence, the legitimacy – of the persuasive strategies employed in some of the examples considered, especially when exploitation is involved of the uncertainties which have arisen round the sense of personal identity in the late-modern world. To concluding by considering this topic a little further, it is useful to return to critical social theory. Both Giddens and Habermas stress the fragile or vulnerable nature of individual identity. Among the features of late modern society identified as potential threats to a stable sense of identity, capable of confronting the individual with 'the looming threat of personal meaninglessness', Giddens (1991a: 201) draws particular attention to the insidious tendency to commodify the project of the self as such, a tendency exacerbated, in his view, by advertising and media entertainment (1991a: 198). More recently, Giddens (1998: 31–6 & 133–4) has confirmed that the accelerating pace of globalisation and information technology and the spread of cultural pluralism and individualist ideologies have intensified such problems. Habermas (1987: 325) also warns of the power of consumerism and possessive individualism to distort communicative practice and promote a utilitarian concept of lifestyle. While rationally-grounded argumentation is fundamental to his concept of ethical discourse, Habermas does recognise a manipulative use of communication, regarding it as something parasitic on communicative action. There is a type of action, that is, classed as strategic and covert, oriented not to reaching understanding but to achieving success (1984: 333), manifested in interactions in which 'one subject inconspicuously harnesses another for his own purposes, that is, induces him to behave in a desired way by manipulatively employing linguistic means and thereby instrumentalizes him for his own success' (1984: 288).

Although much advertising could be placed in the commodifying and manipulative categories discussed above, there is probably no need to take a pessimistic view of the ability of social subjects to resist persuasion. It is true, as we have seen, that the interpretation of advertisements as coherent often seems to depend on the tacit acceptance, on the part of addressees, of certain presupposed norms of evaluation which legitimise the persuasive reasons being presented. It would be as well to recall, however, a point made earlier in this chapter: argumentational coherence does not necessarily go hand in hand with successful persuasion. There is a type of coherence, which we might term critical, which is constructed by understanding – and rejecting – promotional texts as designed to achieve merely self-interested goals, as opposed to discourse oriented to genuinely communicative ones. Such interpretations, furthermore, may well enable us to resist being cast in standardised consumer roles rather than addressed as fully individuated subjects. In conditions of late modernity it behoves us all, perhaps, to expand the traditional warning to buyers: *caveat emptor, caveat persona*.

References

'Toro' in *Condorito de Oro: selección de los mejores chistes,* Panama: Editorial América, 1987.

Bourdieu, P., *Language and Symbolic Power.* (ed. Thompson, J.B., trans. Raymond, G.& Adamson, M.), Cambridge: Polity, 1992.

Cook, G., *The Discourse of Advertising,* London: Routledge, 1992, p. 148.

Crystal, D., *Dictionary of Language and Languages,* Harmondsworth: Penguin, 1994.

de Beaugrande, R., *Text, Process and Discourse,* London: Longman, 1980.

Eemeren, F. & Grootendorst, R., 'The Study of Argumentation from a Speech Act Perspective' in Verscheuren, J. (ed.) *Pragmatics at Issue,* vol. 1, Amsterdam: Benjamin, 1991, pp.151–70.

Eemeren, F. & Grootendorst, R., *Fundamentals of Argumentation Theory,* Mahwah N.J., Erlbaum, 1996, pp. 286–7.

Finn, H., 'Keeping up Appearances', *Financial Times, Weekend,* 10 October 1999.

Giddens, A., *Modernity and Self-Identity,* Cambridge: Polity, 1991a.

Giddens, A., *The Consequences of Modernity,* Cambridge: Polity, 1991b.

Giddens, A., *The Third Way: The Renewal of Social Democracy,* Cambridge: Polity, 1998.

Green, G.M., *Pragmatics and Natural Language Understanding,* Hillsdown N.J.: Erlbaum, 1989, pp. 110–11.

Habermas, J., *The Theory of Communicative Action, Volume 1.,* (trans. McCarthy, T.), London: Heinemann, 1984.

Habermas, J., *The Theory of Communicative Action, Volume 2,.* (trans. McCarthy, T.), Cambridge: Polity, 1987.

Habermas, J., *Moral Consciousness and Communicative Action,* (trans. Lenhardt, C. & Weber Nicholson, S., introduction by McCarthy, T.), Cambridge: Polity, 1990.

Mann, W.C. *et al,* 'Rhetorical Structure Theory and Text Analysis' in Mann, W.C., & Thompson, S.A., *Discourse Description: Diverse Linguistic Analyses of a Fund-Raising Text,* Amsterdam: Benjamin, 1992, p. 58.

Schiffrin, D. 'The Management of a Cooperative Self During Argument: the Role of Opinions and Stories' in Grimshaw, A.D. (ed.), *Conflict Talk,* Cambridge: Cambridge University Press, 1990, pp. 241–59.

Schiffrin, D., *Approaches to Discourse,* Oxford: Blackwell, 1994, p. 371.

Searle, J.R., *Expression and Meaning,* Cambridge: Cambridge University Press, 1979, pp. 30–57.

Sperber, D. & Wilson, D., *Relevance: Communication and Cognition.* 2nd edn, Oxford: Blackwell, 1995, pp. 250–1.

Tannen, D., *Coherence in Spoken and Written Discourse,* Norwood N.J.: Ablex, 1984, pp. xiv.

Tsui, A., 'Sequencing Rules and Coherence in Discourse', *Journal of Pragmatics,* 15 (1991), pp. 11–29.

8 The Dull, the Conventional and the Sexist
Portuguese Wine Advertising

Cristina Água-Mel
Trinity College, Dublin

Introduction

Williams suggested that advertising had become involved with the teaching of social and personal values, in the same way as myths went about providing explanations in the primitive societies (Williams, 1960 & 1980). V. L. Leymore (1975: ix) reinforces this idea by claiming that advertising had in fact replaced myth in modern societies. She says that advertising, like myths in earlier societies, was being used to 'reinforce accepted modes of behaviour'.

One particular area in which advertising has always had an important social function is gender representation. Advertisers like to use images of women, sex and romance because they are 'eye-stoppers' (Packard, 1957: 75). But more than just being attention-grabbers, the gender representations used in advertising also have a strong impact on our social standards. Erving Goffman (1979: 8) says that gender reflects fundamental features of the social structure and as such it can offer, more than class and other social divisions, an understanding of what our ultimate nature is. Vestergaard & Schrøder (1985: 73–4) also believe that the visual and verbal representation of the sexes in advertising stands as a reproduction of our gender identities, and Jhally (1990: 135) goes as far as to say that 'advertisements are part of the whole context within which we understand and define our gender relations' as well as being 'part of the process by which we learn about gender'.

The representation of males and females in commercial advertising has always been fundamentally different. We have come a long way from the traditional representation of women as housewives and of men as providers, but the representation of women in advertising is a misrepresentation of reality: somehow 'advertising has not been able to keep pace with women's changing roles and aspirations' (Dyer, 1982: 185). Winship (1980) believes that even when advertising appears to be producing a *new* representation of femininity, rather than reproducing an already existing one, it does so by relying on patriarchal and capitalist relations. She suggests that women are represented in a fetishistic mode, in which women are allowed to have an active sexuality but only in as much as it is used for the satisfaction of men rather than themselves.

Another feature of present-day advertising is its awareness of its influence and of its critics. One the one hand, it has, for example, taken advantage of a hedonistic trend in which people seek pleasure and escapism and it provides them with exactly that, not only through the use of the product or service advertised but through the ads themselves. On the other hand, advertisers are also aware of the criticisms that have been made in relation to advertising, and have learnt to integrate that criticism into their ads, which have become increasingly playful, parodic and self-referential.

It is this flexibility and permanent change that engages consumers, and in the long run indirectly influences and constructs their view of the world. According to Wernick (1991: 30), 'in order to summon the relevant audience and persuade them to try the product, some ads set out to construct a personal and social identity for its potential users'.

The Portuguese Case

With these general considerations in mind we decided to take a look at advertising in Portugal, and ask what kind of personal and social identity is being constructed for modern men and, more importantly, for modern women. A product strongly embedded in Portuguese culture such as wine was chosen in an attempt to see how much of its advertising relies on already existing cultural background and how much of it attempts to construct a new social identity for both the males and females represented. The analysis is based on a collection of Portuguese wine adverts published in newspapers and magazines during the late 1980s and 1990s. It should also be said that this brief study represents the starting point of a more complete and comparative analysis of different wine advertising. For the purposes of this article I have chosen four examples of Portuguese wine advertising, which stand as samples of what is being published.

Portugal has been a wine producing country since Roman times. Vineyards are found almost everywhere in the country, from the Minho region to the Algarve, from the narrow coastal plains to the high mountains of the interior, as well as Madeira and the Azores, covering a total area of approximately 400,000 hectares. Portuguese governments have always protected and encouraged the spread of this product. Today, the wine industry employs 25% of the working agricultural population. The economic value of wine and the social and cultural importance of viticulture are important factors in the country's economy (ICEP: 2). Data from 1991–7 show that Portugal maintains a high level of internal consumption, although the tendency everywhere else and particularly in other traditional wine-producing countries like France, Spain and Italy is towards a decrease (World Drink Trends). Hence, it is not surprising that the last ten years have witnessed a significant increase in wine advertising, specially in certain types of media, such as the weekend magazines of the Sunday papers, and billboards. This increase is also a result of a stronger, more open competition between the new and traditional ways of wine producing, as well as the opening of the Portuguese frontiers to other wines. Producers have realised that now is the time to start promoting brand loyalty because within the framework of EU free market policies, Portuguese wines have begun to face competition in their own market from more prestigious or cheaper wines from other EU countries. Producers have also understood that there is a large potential consumer segment in the Portuguese wine market that needs to be tackled: the increasing number of young urban consumers, whose drinking habits need to be created, reinforced or even changed.

Marketing Traditional Values

As everywhere in the world, Portuguese wine advertising relies on images of seduction, sociability and sophistication. Wine ads create clear associations between the product and romantic encounters, party celebrations and meals, leisure pursuits and relaxation. In Portuguese wine ads, wine is also projected as 'a symbol of material well-being and contentment' (Unwin, 1991: 349) as well as of status and power.

One particular group of advertisements addresses a more restricted circle of wine consumers and is clearly aimed at the respectable, middle-aged head of the household and relies mostly on 'solid', 'traditional', and 'familiar' signs. Sobriety, respectability, prestige, and tradition are the keynote of these ads, which usually show a wine bottle in a prominent position set against backgrounds frequently connected with the wine characteristics, place of origin or possible contexts of wine consumption. But no matter what image is chosen to illustrate the wine product, none of these ads dares to show anything beyond the realm of wine: the land where it is produced, the wine features or the people who help to make it. In this category of prestige wine advertising, the text gives the extra information that the image alone could not transmit: either an explanation of the objects shown in the picture or a message from the authoritative male interlocutor represented in the picture; advertisements that use a male figure always aim at establishing a bond between the male represented in the ad and the male consumer whose interest is engaged through the image and the information contained in the ad. The final objective of these ads is not to change consumers' habits but to guide their brand choice. This is done by providing the consumer with the additional wine knowledge that will transform him (these ads are always aimed at male buyers) into a wine buff and consequently increase his social prestige.

A clear example of this first type of wine advertisement, using a wine related landscape and a bottle of wine in a predominant position on the page, is the ad for Charamba red wine by Aveleda, published in 1997 in a specialist magazine. This ad has the same features which Odber de Baubeta (1998) observed for some Portuguese advertising – the dependency on the visual impact of the bright colours, an eye-catching layout, bold captions and orthographic puns; simple and direct syntax, an almost telegraphic use of short or fragmented sentences, with hardly any verbs, but with plenty of evocative adjectives, repetitions, hyperboles and resounding non-statements; images of the familiar or scenes from everyday life.

> **Douro.**
> **Prata.**
> Charamba é o novo vinho da Aveleda. Um tinto nascido nas encostas do Douro, mas que já ganhou fama (e prémios) em todo o mundo – Medalha de Prata na VINEEXPO '97 – Bordéus e 86 pontos na revista WINE SPECTATOR. Abra uma garrafa de Charamba e descubra um vinho macio, intenso e muito apreciado.

(Made of Gold.
Silver Medal.
Charamba is the new wine by Aveleda. A red which was born on the slopes of the Douro
mountains, but that has already won fame (and prizes) all over the world – a silver medal
in the VINEEXPO '97 – Bordeaux and 86 points from the WINE SPECTATOR magazine.
Open a bottle of Charamba and discover a soft, intense and much appreciated wine.)

In this ad the 'visual impact of the bright colours' has been replaced by a single but
predominant red wine colour which dominates the entire page lending the
photographic image an aura of beauty and warmth. The layout is also very clever: the
landscape is on the top right, the textual elements guiding the reader's eyes to the right
of the page towards the highlighted bottle, standing upright on the right-hand side of
the picture and hence in the most prominent position on the page. The bright red
colour reflected by the light that illuminates the bottle creates a 'natural' division
between the upper part of the ad and that containing the text. The background image
is certainly one familiar to every Portuguese person, not only because of its natural
beauty but because of its world-famous wine slopes. The Douro valley is probably the
landscape most immediately recognised and associated with wine in Portugal, and yet,
and although the metaphor is quite obvious, the text insists on spelling it out: 'Um
tinto nascido nas encostas do Douro.'

The catchphrase in this ad is both a pun and a play on words: it is a phonetic
metonymic pun in which the words 'Ouro' (gold) and 'Prata' (silver) are used instead
of 'medalha de ouro' and 'medalha de prata', and it plays with the name of the river,
Douro, and 'de ouro', 'made of gold' or 'a gold medal', followed by a silver medal:
'prata', in direct reference to a silver medal won by this wine in an international
competition. The name of the wine is repeated three times and so is the wine-
producing company: Aveleda, featured once on the bottle's label and twice in the text.

In Portuguese wine advertising it is also usual to find advertisements that present
an expert or some prestigious male figure directly addressing the consumer. This
approach was used recurrently by Sogrape in the early 1990s. The following ad is for
José de Sousa, a wine produced in the Alentejo, famous for its red, and also the first
wine region in the country to modernise its wine-producing facilities and bring in
scientists to improve the wine-making process.

Do amor ao detalhe nasce um grande vinho... José de Sousa, em potes de barro.

(A great wine is born out of detail... José de Sousa, in clay pots)

This ad shows the oenologist who works for the wine company in 'mangas de camisa',
with his sleeves rolled up to do his work, holding a tasting glass of red wine. His name
and function in the company are stated underneath the picture: 'Domingo Soares
Franco, Enólogo de José Maria da Fonseca'. But what is important is what is behind
him: the 'potes de barro' in which this wine is fermented. The text tells a story that
corroborates the main theme of the ad, that a great wine is born from attention to

detail, 'detalhe'. The wordplay continues between 'detalhe' (de - talhe) and 'talhas' or 'potes de barro' – the large clay pots common in that part of the country. The copywriter has used terminology known only to people from the Alentejo or to wine connoisseurs. This ad, published in the *Expresso* colour supplement, is not aimed at new buyers but instead at the wine buyer who might consider buying a different brand, if 'talked into it'.

Marketing the New Consumers' Habits

Another category of Portuguese wine advertisements aims at changing consumers' drinking habits, or attracting new market segments. The target audience for these ads is again male, but younger and probably urban. Unlike the previous ads where it is assumed that the reader is already interested in the product, these advertisements have to grab the consumers' attention at the initial stages. This is probably the reason why the images are more varied, attractive and striking than in the ads mentioned above. Their most common images are of seduction, social enjoyment or relaxation. The main objective of the advertising message is no longer to be informative, but to suggest new environments, new situations, new reasons for consuming wine. The text, sometimes a single sentence, links the already suggestive image to a possible meaning. In this way it guides the reader according to the intentions of the advertisers.

Although more innovative than those described above, the ads that follow under this category retain the same features as conventional advertising. An example of this is the Sogrape's Mateus Rosé ad: 'Paula'. Sogrape is one of the most important wine producers in Portugal and it has sponsored a few very sophisticated and creative/innovative wine campaigns. Their 'Mateus' rosé wine was the first Portuguese wine, after Port wine, to be exported and gain worldwide acclaim after a strong marketing campaign in foreign markets, so it is only natural that they should use similar techniques to increase their sales within Portugal. Most of the Mateus Rosé ads try to establish positive associations between the wine and modern society, suggesting new environments where this wine can be consumed. This is in itself an innovation within Portuguese wine advertising, but Sogrape goes even further. Their ad for June 1996 both depicts and describes a woman in a workplace, as well as trying to establish a link between this type of wine and birthday celebrations. The role of the wine buyer is still being assigned to the male, but the woman is given a personality and is transported to a central position in the advertisement's message.

The image illustrates the narrative and shows Paula at the moment when her colleagues come into her office and start to sing 'Happy Birthday', toasting her birthday with Mateus Rosé. Her hands are covering her cheeks as she blushes, turning pink because that is the colour of the wine. The whole ad plays with two important and striking features of this type of wine: its colour pink and the shape of the bottle. The strong pink colour of the ad and the action of blushing all relate to the wine colour. The text shape and the repetition of the word 'forma' represents an obvious association with the bottle's unusual shape.

It is particularly interesting to observe that although Paula is a modern career woman, possibly high up in the office hierarchy since she has her own office, she is featured as having to play a role of innocence, modesty and submission. The romantic involvement is also represented by the presence of a man immediately behind her, once again because within a more conservative, traditional approach to female representation, a woman is not complete without it.

Most remarkable in this ad is the double visual metaphor. Advertisers often try to connect their brands to positive concepts through the use of comparisons, mostly metaphors, since the use of comparative advertising is illegal in many countries. They do this not only because images have more impact than text, but also because they stay longer in the memory of the consumer. Advertisers also like to use metaphors because the consumer believes he is one of a special minority who understands them, thus creating a favourable complicity between consumer and advertiser. According to Sean Brierley (1995: 146–7), metaphors are an effective method of communication, because they are part of everyday language and also because they bestow meanings on goods. They work by transferring the feelings, emotions and images from one set of objects to a brand, or by associating certain objects with the brand.

Forceville (1996) developed a theory around the visual metaphors present in advertising. He defined the two elements as a 'literal primary subject' and a 'figurative secondary subject' both of which can belong to the domain of meaning elements: facts, connotations, beliefs and attitudes. According to Forceville the similarity between the two elements is most likely created by the metaphor itself. He identifies four types of visual metaphor, according to the associations established inside the advertising image. In the first type the visual metaphor is rendered by one pictorial term; in the second there are two pictorial terms present; in the third type the metaphor is rather more like a simile; and finally in the fourth type of metaphor one of the terms is rendered pictorially and the other verbally.

The Mateus Rosé ad on page 82 is a clear example of this fourth type of verbo-pictorial metaphor. The textual element is crucial for the understanding of the pictorial subject; it guides the reader towards the meaning the advertiser intended, but the text also imitates the bottle shape. In this ad the text serves a primary function, which Forceville has defined as that of 'anchoring' the image, but it also bears a *'formal resemblance'* to the product itself. The metaphor exists at two levels of interpretation: the literal connection between text and image, as well as the conceptual metaphor between text and product, and because this is placed centrally on the page it is of crucial importance for the full reading of the ad.

A final type of Portuguese wine advertising also belonging to this verbo-pictorial category is one which uses the clear associations between wine and seduction. In this kind of ad, the advertisers may also suggest new environments in which their product may be consumed, but the main message is one of sexual desire of men for women. The women represented in these ads are usually pictured as passive, easily captured by the seductive powers of men and the wine they buy for them. The following example was published in August 1996 in *Notícias Magazine* and it shows a moment of intimacy moment between a heterosexual couple. The black and white photographic image pictures a woman and a man beside her looking her straight in the eyes. One of her hands is supporting her head, which is slightly inclined. According to Goffman (1979:

Paula estava
passada.
Um dia inteiro
e ninguém
se lembrara.
**Ela tinha
até dado**
algumas pistas
como, por exemplo,
o quanto adorava

o cor-de-rosa.

Mas nada! Melhor desistir, pensou,
com um arzinho triste. E foi nesse exacto
momento que os colegas invadiram o seu escritório,

erguendo os copos de Mateus.

Sur-pre-sa! Enquanto eles cantavam os parabéns,
Paula sentiu as faces a ficarem rosadas. Levou as mãos ao rosto.
Ao menos devo estar a combinar com a cor do copo,

foi o que pensou. E desatou a rir.

Afinal, o dia do seu aniversário começava a ter a forma

que ela tanto desejara.

Mateus   A SUA FORMA DE VIVER.

(Paula was mad. A whole day and no one had remembered. She had even dropped some hints about, for example, how much she loved the colour pink. But no! Better to give up, she thought, pouting a little bit. But it was at that exact moment that her colleagues invaded her office, raising their glasses of Mateus. Sur-pri-se! While they were singing Happy Birthday, Paula's cheeks turned pink. She tried to hide it with her hands. At least I'm matching the colour of the wine, she thought, and started to laugh. In the end, her birthday was beginning to have the shape she had always wanted. Mateus, YOUR WAY OF LIVING.)

46) this position 'can be read as an acceptance of subordination, an expression of ingratiation, submissiveness and appeasement'. In the Portuguese ad the woman is drinking from a glass that she 'delicately' holds by the stem. She is looking straight back at him, with a seductive, insinuating gaze. He is holding the stem of the glass which rests on the table. They are very close together, suggesting intimacy, romance

and sexual attraction. In the foreground of the picture, to the right, in a different scale and in colour, is a large bucket full of ice cubes in which lies a bottle of Aveleda wine.

[Apostamos que ela se derrete antes do gelo]. Aveleda Fonte. Sobe ao coração.

([We bet she'll melt before the ice.] Aveleda Fountain. Goes straight to the heart.)

The text is simple and consists of a single sentence in brackets, as if it were a whisper or an aside by a third person standing outside the picture voyeuristically watching the couple and making a guess as to what is going to happen next. Asides are a very common feature of Portuguese comedy and theatre. The use of the verb 'derreter-se' creates a strong double meaning since this verb means 'to melt' but also has the figurative sense of 'falling for someone'. The text inside the brackets can also be read as someone else making a bet on the outcome of a romantic encounter. The verb form presents a first-person plural, which in Portuguese can also be used as a neutral form. Here the 'we' is extremely ambiguous, as it might represent the wine producers/advertisers, or a group of people standing outside the picture and commenting. Either way it will involve the male reader in the seduction that it is going on, by either responding to the challenge made by the producers of this wine/advertisers or by becoming part of the group observing/making this bet and thereby identifying with the man in the picture.

The connection between image and text is not one of explanation or 'anchorage' but rather one of suggestion, and yet it creates a relationship between the ad and its audience. There is no direct command telling the consumer to buy this wine yet there is a challenge that a male reader will be tempted to meet. The ad has one final sentence which explains how the male represented in the picture will win this bet: because the wine he has bought her will go straight to her heart (rather then her head), she will be won over by his personality, method of seduction or choice of wine, and she will 'melt' or fall in love. Seduction is the key word, being expressed both in the image and in the text, but there is also an appeal to more lasting sentiments of love. This light sparkling wine has gained the qualities of a magic love potion and can help the male, as he will be traditionally the one choosing and buying the wine, to seduce the female.

However, this wine ad, like the other examples described above, has not taken account of the habits of modern women. It is still relying on the portrayal of the passive, submissive and obliging female to whom Winship (1980) refers as being representative of the way women are characterised in modern advertising.

Conclusion

The first two examples of wine adverts analysed make it clear that Portuguese wine advertising still depends on widely held myths and stereotypical ideas surrounding wine and its consumption to sell the product. Because these myths and representations are already present in the consumers' minds, the advertisers only need to make a simple connection between product and consumer, one that relies on traditional values and conservatism, represented in the advertising texts and images by typically

Portuguese landscapes or even a 'man to man' talk. The structures and characteristics of the wine consumer are not being 'constructed' but maintained and reinforced. Portuguese wine advertising is not aiming at the creation of a new wine consumer but rather at reassuring its audience of the prevalence of tradition and old customs. In a changing society, even when such change is slow, there are many people who need to be told that the establishment is still good, and that they will not have to change. Advertising tells people what they want to hear and even when advertisers attempt to alter consumers' behaviour, they will do so by presenting a solid basis of prevalent beliefs, followed by an almost subliminal suggestion of a possible change.

The other two ads presented on this analysis were rather more interesting in that they were aimed at the new young and urban wine consumer. Yet the gender representations used in either one of them was one also based on traditional codes of how women should behave socially. These ads, just as the previous ones, were not addressing women but men, and although women seem to be at the centre of these ads, it is only because they are the object of the male desire, awaiting to be 'conquered' (i.e. surprised or 'melted') through some magic love portion (i.e. wine) given to them by a male figure.

These gender representations do not reflect the state of Portuguese society and, more importantly, women's position in that society, and yet they are still being used. The majority of Portuguese women now work outside the home, and an equally large percentage of women are financially independent. Nonetheless, wine ads continue to be aimed mainly at men with women being represented as mere objects, having to behave in a lady-like way, still dependent on male approval.

References

Brierley, S., *The Advertising Handbook*, London: Routledge, 1995.

Dyer, G., *Advertising as Communication*, London: Methuen, 1982.

Forceville, C., *Pictorial Metaphor in Advertising*, London: Routledge, 1996.

Goffman, E., *Gender Advertisements*, London: Macmillan, 1979, p. 46.

ICEP, 'Investimentos, Comércio e Turismo de Portugal' in *Wines of Portugal*, p. 2.

Jhally, S., *The Codes of Advertising – Fetishism and the Political Economy of Meaning in the Consumer Society*, London: Routledge, 1990, p 135.

Leymore, V.L., *Hidden Myth, Structure and Symbolism in Advertising*, New York: Basic Books Inc. Publishers, 1975.

Odber de Baubeta, P.A., 'The Language of Advertising in Portugal', *Vida Hispánica*, 37 (1988), pp. 40–6.

Packard, V., *The Hidden Persuaders*, Harmondsworth: Penguin, 1957.

Unwin, T., *Wine and the Vine; an historical geography of viticulture and the wine trade*, London: Routledge, 1991.

Vestergaard, T. & Schrøder K., *The Language of Advertising*, Oxford: Blackwell, 1985.

Wernick, A., *Promotional Culture – advertising, ideology and symbolic expression*, London: Sage, 1991.

Williams, R., 'Advertising: Magic System' in *Problems in Materialism and Culture*, London: Verso, 1980.

Williams, R., 'The Magic System' in *New Left Review*, 4 (1960), pp. 27–32.

Winship, J., 'Sexuality for Sale' in Hall, S., Hobson, D., Lowe, A. & Wills, P. (eds.) *Culture, Media, Language*, London: Hutchinson, 1980.

World Drink Trends, NTC Publications Ltd. in association with Produktschap Voor Gedistilleerde Dranken.

9 Spreading the Word and Sticking Your Tongue Out

The Dual Rhetoric of Language Advertising in Catalan

Helena Buffery
University of Birmingham

The study of advertising has proved a fertile field for semioticians and discourse analysts, seeking to gauge the factors involved in the construction of social meaning. Yet there has been relatively little focus on the use of advertising in language planning, on the ways in which language advertising has been employed to create cultural cohesion. Where studies exist they tend to be of a descriptive nature, such as the documented record of the Campaign for Linguistic Normalisation in Catalonia (Departament de Cultura, 1983), or else they seek to evaluate the success of particular campaigns in the implementation of linguistic policy (Strubell i Trueta, 1992). Lack of attention to the role, let alone the rhetoric, of language advertising reflects a tendency to prioritise the visual in semiotic analyses of contemporary cultural forms, and a narrow definition of communication in some linguistic analyses. Part of the problem stems from the difficulties in disentangling the big business side of advertising from its social effects and interaction (Costa, 1993). In effect, the globalisation of economic markets and the multinational campaigns that constitute their most public face is inseparable from the steady instrumentalisation of language, as a tool for communicating desire or exchange value. As Benavides Delgado (1997: 290) observes, the hegemony of advertising is now such that it constructs the values used by individuals and social groups in their everyday lives. Current focus on the relationship between advertising and identity, and the diverse forms of identification on which advertising depends, presents a response to this changing context, a response that frames the study I have undertaken here. In many ways, however, the campaigns I have chosen to discuss could not be further removed from contemporary market trends. The promotion of Catalan in the Catalan-speaking regions of Spain might appear to appeal to a limited public, of only minor relevance to current studies of advertising. Nevertheless, it is of wider interest because, notwithstanding the limited geographical sphere of its operation, the campaigns self-consciously both had to create a public appeal and market the product, a product which was also to be the instrument of its own promotion. The very indeterminacy of the meaning of 'Catalan' for the inhabitants of Catalonia, reflected in its dual status within the campaigns themselves,

85

informs the rhetorical strategies employed to position the target audience. The social and political context into which the Normalisation – *Norma* – campaign was introduced also affected the rhetorical positions incorporated in its discourse. The strong ideological basis of political Catalanism in the relationship between language and identity necessitated the promotion of Catalan as a way of guaranteeing the democratic rights of Catalan-speaking subjects. However, the campaign also needed to convince the audience of the relationship between language and identity and hence contained the underlying aim of changing attitudes to language and linguistic conduct. To study the *Norma* campaign of 1982–3 is to encounter a multi-layered narrative, combining different linguistic knowledges with different understandings of language. By promoting the same thing as many different things, the campaign ultimately called for different levels of identification with its content, seeking to represent a diversity of identity positions within what was consistently expressed as a collective project. In the world of language planning, at least, that area of linguistics dedicated to the formulation and implementation of linguistic policies, it has become one of the most influential advertising campaigns of the last quarter of a century (Departament de Cultura, 1983:72).

In Catalonia, where the make-up of the Catalan-speaking public had changed enormously over the Franco years, the necessity of a campaign to prepare for linguistic normalisation (the promotion of Catalan in the public sphere) in the wake of the autonomous elections of 1980 became clear. One of the principle aims of the Franco regime had been to implant national unity, in terms of language, culture and religion, and so Catalonia had suffered a concerted campaign to eradicate any sign of difference. The Catalan language was banned from the public sphere, manifestations of Catalan culture suppressed or re-appropriated as part of national folklore, and the history of the language presented as that of a regional dialect of Spain. Although the Spanish Constitution of 1978 sought to represent once more the plurality of identities that constitute present-day Spain, the question of how these identities could be represented and would be interrelated remained unclear. The majority recognition of Catalan as a symbol of Catalan identity, and the democratic election of a Catalan party to the leadership of the reconstituted Generalitat in 1980 did not resolve entirely these problems in the region. When Josep Tarradellas (the President of the Generalitat in exile) arrived in Barcelona in 1977, he announced his arrival with 'Ciutadans de Catalunya, ja sóc aquí' (Citizens of Catalonia, I have returned), hence drawing attention to the continuing question of the identity of the inhabitants of Catalonia. In the build up to the referendum on the Statute of Autonomy and the Generalitat elections, there was inter-party support for the following slogans of inclusion: 'Ara més que mai, un sol poble' (Now, more than ever, a single people) and 'Es català tothom qui viu i treballa a Catalunya' (Everyone who lives and works in Catalonia is a Catalan). Large numbers of non-Catalan speakers had moved to Catalonia under the dictatorship, and equally great were the numbers of Catalan speakers who had never learned to write their language. The extent and depth of acceptance of a Catalan identity once the common enemy, in the person of Franco, had been removed could not be taken for granted. In fact, that a language and culture so proscribed by the needs of the Nation State should have become one of the exemplary models of regional identity in the 1990s might appear, to foreign eyes, to be a minor miracle (Báez de Aguilar González, 1997: 21). The change did not happen overnight, however, and there is ample documentation of the campaigns devised in the 1980s to educate and influence the inhabitants of Catalonia in their perception of language and, hence, of Catalan. What is more, the Generalitat today continues to be circumspect about the role of advertising in modern culture: to ensure the continued utility of Catalan, it must be made into a viable language of advertising.

My aim here is to consider the rhetoric used in 'selling' Catalan over the past two decades, to explore how the strategies employed reflect the interpellations intended by the language planners. By showing its relationship to earlier discourse on the relationship between language and identity, I hope to suggest how and why advertising might have contributed to the current shift in focus of the debate over the Catalan language. For notwithstanding the fact that Catalonia is now recognised internationally as a region with an identity distinct from that of the rest of Spain, there is much dissent nationally, and within the region itself, concerning the legitimacy of recent linguistic policies (Santamaria, 1999). The juxtaposition of old and new common to language advertising in the Catalan-speaking regions provides the framework for my study, ranging between the nineteenth-century associations of 'Catalanitat' with 'el Verb Català' (the Catalan Word) and more recent slogans of tongue-twisting defiance, as devised in the Illes Balears. Examples of the persistence of a traditionalist rhetoric, linking Catalan identity to the land and rural customs, include the localised use of 'auques' (traditional story-forms mingling visual vignettes with short captions) to tell the story of the Catalan language, and the appeal to rural images such as the Catalan 'pagès' (farmer), or the 'pastorets' (popular Christmas plays based on figures from the Nativity) in non-urban areas. The polysemy of the word 'llengua' (language, but also tongue) has resulted in more contemporary slogans of sociolinguistic exhortation, such as 'Treu la llengua' ('Stick your tongue out', but also 'Bring out your language') and 'No et mosseguis la llenga' ('Don't bite your tongue', but also 'Don't hold back or harm your language'), both of which were used by the Generalitat Balear in the 1980s. It is a juxtaposition that we might trace to the widely-perceived divergences in the nineteenth-century roots of contemporary Catalan nationalism: between the vision of a 'modern bourgeois Catalonia with a personality defined not by tradition but by urban political progress' and the 'Catholic conservatism of the Catalan countryside' (Woolard, 1989: 24). Beginning by setting the most high-profile campaign for the promotion of Catalan in context, I will proceed to describe its rhetorical operation before reflecting on its effects in 1990s Catalonia.

The campaign that is the primary focus of my study made its first public appearance, for the benefit of representatives of the local administrations in Catalonia, in October 1981. Its context is that of the post-Franco debate over the linguistic rights of the regional autonomies and of Castilian speakers in the 'new' Spain. The early 1980s saw increasing division in the Cortes and in the press, resulting in the 'Manifiesto' of Spanish-speaking intellectuals in Catalonia, and the F-23 coup in February 1981, whose principle catalyst was thought to be military discomfort about the break-up of Spain.

Faced with such a volatile political situation, any project that sought to promote the linguistic rights of Catalan speakers, as officially guaranteed by the recently redrawn Spanish Constitution, would require a conciliatory message. Everything about the campaign points to such an aim. In fact, the decisions taken have been carefully recorded, partly because of some adverse reactions, although none of these, it is claimed, came from Castilian speakers (Departament de Cultura, 1983: 9–17). What the campaign set out to sell was Catalan – as a 'cosa de tots'. 'Tots' was chosen rather than 'tothom', to suggest a collectivity of individuals, rather than everyone being the same.

Catalan needed to be sold at this time in preparation for the coming Linguistic Normalisation drive and the 1983 Law, whereby the Generalitat would fund language programmes and other projects to increase the use of Catalan in the region. Ultimately Catalan would have to become a language of advertising, too, and hence the material possibility of the campaign is in many ways part of the process of selling Catalan. To sell linguistic normalisation in a region where many citizens did not speak Catalan, and where speakers did not necessarily have the ability to write the language, obviously necessitated an all-embracing rhetoric, but also a rhetoric that did not suggest imperialist assimilation or imposition. Current visions of a nationalist assimilationist movement in Catalan culture fail to acknowledge the fact that Catalans in the 1970s and 1980s were very sensitive about this very issue; a sensitivity that is reflected in a certain intellectual distancing from early twentieth-century *Noucentista* discourse, with its cultural imperialist flavour. Ironically, if we study texts produced in the post-Franco years, including the advertising campaigns, there are many links and echoes of past discourses, but these remainders are of a universalising tendency rather than overt signs of cultural protectionism. So the normalisation drive was embodied in the figure of La Norma, who represented the Norm, short for Normalisation, with direct reference to Fabra's grammatical *Normes* of the beginning of the century (Fabra, 1913). Yet La Norma was also simply a girl's name, all names in Catalan requiring the use of the definite article except in situations of direct address. Norma was represented as a child, something unthreatening, innocent and open; with the explicit intention that she be able to come out with home truths without offending anyone (Departament de Cultura, 1983: 15). Norma represented the children who were now officially required to learn Catalan at school; she represented hope for the future. Yet Norma also belongs to a more problematic tradition of representation; that of the use of idealised female figures to represent the future of Catalonia and its rootedness in the past – as muses for the 'men' of action. Such a tradition can be traced back to Eugeni d'Ors' 'La ben plantada' of the 1910s, embodying the desired values for a civilised Catalonia. The use of a child also invokes the famous symbol of collective action of the Civil War period, in the cartoon Republican boy 'El més petit de tots'.

The focus of the campaign on cultural cohesion, on the regulation of linguistic conduct, and so primarily on legitimising bilingual conversations, might seem to fit in with general perceptions, particularly today, of a certain imperialism in Catalan culture, of a tendency towards assimilation and exclusion, of artificial intervention to impose a specific model of subjectivity. A model which has – if we are to believe the right-wing newpaper *ABC* – created a kind of subaltern class of Castilian speakers in

Catalonia, oppressed by the need to use Catalan. However, statistical studies present a rather different picture, in which the campaign and others like it did indeed produce a high degree of consensus. Responses from all sections of society were positive; Norma was well received all over Catalonia and feted in other regions (such as the Basque Country, where the campaign was imitated) and in international symposia; and by the end of the 1980s above 90% of the population accepted Catalan, reporting that they could understand it. Yet the outcome of the campaign in more general terms is unclear, particularly *vis-à-vis* the creation of social cohesion and community, and the direction of future campaigns remains unclear. After the euphoria of the post-1986 census 'Som sis milions' (There are six million of us) campaign, it was discovered that the figures might be deceptive. In preparing his own study of the sociolinguistic situation in greater Barcelona, Báez de Aguilar (1997) draws attention to the divergences between the statistical corpora produced since 1986. His own findings, whilst failing to uncover any overt hostility of the type detected in some of Woolard's (1989) respondents, show a high level of ambiguity in attitudes to Catalan and the question of linguistic consciousness, and growing suspicion as to the direction of future language policy. Most campaigns in the 1990s that have been aimed at the whole community, rather than identifying specific sectors such as the unions, have tended to appeal to a sense of place as a symbol of identity, and particularly to the potent trope of Barcelona. It is to be noted that these campaigns, such as 'Barcelona, posa't maca' (Barcelona, do yourself up) and 'Barcelona més que mai' (Barcelona, more than ever) originated in the Ajuntament (Town Hall) rather than the Generalitat. As has been seen in the 1999 elections the political make-up of the city of Barcelona does not reflect that of the traditional Catalanist strongholds of the rest of Catalonia, in particular the North.

In order to discuss the complexities of the market situation created, the different representational models that proliferated, and the wider question of language (and particularly minority language) in advertising, it is necessary to address in more detail the rhetoric of language advertising: the diversity of strategies used, and of negotiations produced in Catalan-speaking areas. Ideally, this would require a three-pronged approach: 1) to analyse the rhetoric of language advertising and how it attempts to convince of the relationship between language and identity in Catalonia and in the Països Catalans; 2) to assess the national and international dimensions of this advertising and its reception, in relation to global perceptions of the relationship between language and identity; 3) to attempt to characterise Catalan in terms of global advertising, identifying what kind of commodity it has become, and what kind of medium it provides for contemporary publicity.

Here I will concentrate on the first question, although I will include more general observations on the latter two. In analysing the rhetoric of Catalan language advertisements, I shall focus primarily on the system of figures employed by successive campaigns, although it goes without saying that my subject also depends on another sense of rhetoric: rhetoric as persuasion. This blurring of the two senses of rhetoric is one of the key features of the argumentation process employed in Catalan language advertising. For the very use of Catalan is to be seen as purposeful, as a

89

rhetorical position instrumental in the construction of identity, and depends on the acceptance of something (a 'cosa') irreducible in language, something beyond communication. This mythic quality would be associated by sociolinguists such as Lamuela (1996) with the symbolic function of language, ranging from the different attributions of value given to different linguistic forms to the connotations of identity through which speakers identify with their language or their way of speaking – but also if we follow theorists such as Benjamin (1923), the remainder in language that defies translation. The use of 'cosa' in the 1982–3 campaign can be seen as a deliberate attempt to reconcile the forms and usage of Catalan with the linguistic consciousness that produces affective relationships between language and identity. Because of the persecution of Catalan in the public space under Franco, these three different aspects of the language – formal system, social usage and linguistic consciousness – had been split apart.

The slogan 'cosa de tots' seems to be intended primarily to promote social consensus. It is also an easily replaceable signifier, implying the usefulness and functionality of Catalan, and gives the sense of a thing, a possession, of something that is in everybody's interest. 'Cosa de tots' implies an object that belongs to everyone rather than merely a tool for social expression. Hence it is linked on both levels of rhetoric to the persuasion and performance of identity. In unpacking such a simple phrase we may begin to detect its roots in the atmosphere of social unity and intellectual accord between different positions on language and identity crucial to the period after Franco's death (Vilarós, 1999), in which the 1976 Primer Congrés de la Cultura Catalana mirrors the 1906 Primer Congrés de la Llengua Catalana in uniting forces behind the normalisation plan. The activism and defiance of Catalanist rhetoric under Franco is united with the more conservative goals and rhetoric of more dominant groups in recognition of the social changes that had been experienced and in an attempt to second guess (and most probably shape) those to come. In the spirit of democracy, then, the main rhetorical frame is that of consensus – following the solidarity of the 1970s – of Catalan as 'cosa de tots'. However, the apparently 'unified' message of the 1982–3 campaign is also undermined and fragmented, by the employment of diverse forms of address and the differential employment of Catalan and Castilian. One clear example comes in the form of those posters and flyers in which the aims of the campaign are explained to all alongside the meaning of normalisation.

The part of the campaign which focused on changing linguistic conduct made use of cartoon strips and short television broadcasts in which Norma would express her own feelings about Catalan, her attitudes to other speakers, and her evangelical model of linguistic conduct. The narrative voice of a child in such examples suggests an emotional and ethical argumentation process, in contrast to the logical tone of the leaflet reproduced above, which allows her to take on different roles: as actor, as teacher, switching allegiances, showing defiance and outrage but also empathy and kindness. Radio broadcasts, in contrast, represented various everyday situations in which Catalan speakers are encouraged by Castilian speakers to hold bilingual conversations, or Catalan speakers correct each other naturally when non-normative words or phrases (usually borrowings or calques from Castilian) are introduced into the conversation they are holding.

The message is made interactive, as a story to be followed, but also using other material paraphernalia such as stickers. Schools are encouraged to send in their responses, and in particular local administrations are urged to participate in the campaign, producing their own text tailored to the needs of their communities.

Hence the message about Catalan being a 'cosa de tots' is put into action, and it produces further changes in framing and rhetoric depending on the geographical area or social group concerned. One of the free papers distributed in Girona depicts an abstract cityscape in which the inhabitants are busy 're-catalanising' the street signs, with representatives of different age groups and professions putting together the slogan 'El català, feina de tots' in the foreground. A poster produced in Torrelló, in contrast, represents a rural scene, with a pipe-smoking, cap-wearing farm worker contemplating his home town. The slogan here is 'Si Torrelló vols conservar, parla el català' (If you want to conserve Torrelló, speak Catalan). In the comic strips, forms of address change according to the situation: La Norma speaks to the reader of her own personal opinions, although usually without using any form of direct address; we see her in action with Catalan- and Castilian-speaking friends as she encounters different sociocultural contexts; and she uses the second person plural when addressing issues of identity and a collective project. Rarely does she address the reader using second person singular or plural. The examples are hence distanced, not associated with the Catalan-speaking reader, and this ultimately might be seen as promoting an underlying rhetoric of separation and distinction rather than consensus. The visual images used, simple and easily reproduced, again suggest simplicity, homely values and nostalgia, evoking something unthreatening, something fragile that needs help.

In later campaigns of the 1980s the old-fashioned, slightly homely style remains, keying into the 'cosa de tots' rhetoric. More high-tech images are used for the world of industry and commerce, and Catalonia's image projected to the outside world is far more sophisticated in packaging. This can be seen in the target publications for the 'Do you know where Catalonia is?' campaign before the Barcelona Olympics in 1992. Advertisements appeared in the broadsheets in the UK and *Time* and *Newsweek* in the United States. Later campaigns tend to focus more on the utility of language, although the important role of children learning at school remains. In general we see a move towards more impersonal address forms, and increasing wordplay. This tendency reflects greater focus on the utility of Catalan rather than promoting it as a form of identity to be embraced by all. Effectively, there is a rhetorical shift from representations of Catalan as a 'feina de tots' (everyone's business) to an 'eina de feina' (a tool for business). Differential messages depend on the market identified for specific campaigns, reflecting Generalitat targetting of specific sectors, such as the catering world, with high impact on the population as a whole. Yet the changes in rhetoric also reflect the changing sociolinguistic context, with increasing use of Catalan in the education system, and the passing of laws to defend the rights of Catalan speakers. Although the 1990s brought an increasing trend towards individualised messages for particular sectors, with less of an emphasis on consensus, the latter still remains part of the slogans. In a similar manner, the increasing focus on the functional communicative advantages of Catalan, its usefulness in certain sectors, has not completely overtaken more traditional and nostalgic representations – such as the 'auques' produced by certain local authorities. Almost every rhetorical possibility is covered, the sense of consensus allowing for innumerable internal differences. Again this could be linked to the dual action of the 'cosa de tots' slogan.

Most statistics show Castilian speakers to have no preference about which language is used for advertising other commodities (Aguilera, 1995). The question of the utility of Catalan, then, does not seem to create conflictual linguistic consciousness. If there is a conflict, which the extent of debate on the issue of linguistic rights would suggest is the case, then the cause would appear to lie elsewhere. Does the diversity of messages for different regions ultimately suggest a lack of planning, as Lamuela (1996) would probably have it? Or is it a sign of recognition of the complex reality of the Països Catalans, allowing for a variety of sense of identity in linguistic terms? Rather more problematically, where differentiation takes place, it often represents the naivety of the Castilian speaker, the passivity of too many Catalans, and is often framed by archaic and exclusive rhetoric. Although many companies do not use Catalan in advertising for fear of what the rest of Spain might think, there is no doubt that the inhabitants of Catalonia have been made more attuned to the process of persuasion involved in advertising by such campaigns due to Catalan television channels. The commodification of Catalan by the language planners may have contributed to confusion about what exactly it stands for today, but the very process of spreading the word, and the indeterminacy of the rhetoric used to do so, has sealed the effectiveness of sticking one's tongue out – i.e. of using Catalan – whatever the meaning attached to such an act.

References

Aguilera, M.M, and J.M. Romaní, *Actituds dels consumidors davant de l'ús comercial del català*, Barcelona: Generalitat de Catalunya-Departament de Cultura, 1995.

Báez de Aguilar González, F., *El conflicto lingüístico de los emigrantes castellanohablantes en Barcelona*, Málaga: Universidad de Málaga, 1997.

Benavides Delgado, J., *Lenguaje publicitario*, Madrid: Editorial Síntesis, 1997.

Benjamin, W., 'The Task of the Translator' (tr. by Zohn, H.) in Arendt, H. (ed.), *Illuminations*, London: Fontana, 1992, pp. 70–82.

Costa, J., *Reinventar la publicidad*, Madrid: Fundesco, 1993.

Departament de Cultura, *La Campanya per la normalització lingüística de Catalunya*, Barcelona: Generalitat de Catalunya-Departament de Cultura, 1983.

Fabra, P., *Normes*, 1913.

Lamuela, X and Monteagudo, 'Planificación lingüística', in Fernández Pérez, M. (ed.) *Avances en lingüística aplicada*, Santiago de Compostela: Universidad de Santiago de Compostela, 1996, pp. 229–301.

Santamaria, A. (ed.), *Foro Babel. El nacionalismo y las lenguas de Cataluña*, Barcelona: Ediciones Altera, 1999.

Strubell i Trueta, M., 'Les campanyes de normalització lingüística de la Generalitat de Catalunya: 1980–1990', *Revista de Llengua i Dret*, 18 (1992), pp. 181–92

Vilarós, T., 'A Cultural Mapping of Catalonia', in Gies, D. (ed.), *The Cambridge Companion to Modern Spanish Culture*, Cambridge: Cambridge University Press, 1999, pp. 36–53.

Woolard, K., *Double Talk. Bilingualism and the Politics of Ethnicity in Catalonia*, Stanford: Stanford University Press, 1989.

10 Discovering Advertising

Patricia Odber de Baubeta
University of Birmingham

Introduction

As we begin a new millennium, it is interesting to consider some of the images and language that advertisers employ in order to transmit their informative or persuasive messages more effectively. While these are many and varied, certain themes and motifs do stand out, mainly because of the apparent frequency with which they continue to be used. I qualify this statement, because advertising output is notoriously difficult to monitor and quantify. While it might be viable to follow one or more publications for six months or a year, this scrutiny would not offer any assurances regarding the nature and contents of those advertisements published unless we examined a specialist or trade publication such as, for instance, *The British Baker* or *The Grocer*. Advertising is permanently subject to a series of constraints, including prevailing market forces, company budgets and publishers' deadlines. In this context, assembling a thematically coherent corpus of advertisements is often a matter of good fortune or happy coincidence. Nevertheless, certain topics are so deeply embedded in Western European culture, it is neither difficult nor unusual to find examples of them in advertisements published in the print media or shown on television.

Cultural Iconicity and the Discoveries

One topic that has not yet been exhausted by copywriters and advertisers belongs to the deliberately broad category I term 'Cultural iconicity and the Discoveries'. It is recognisable in some British advertising as reminiscent of a colonial past which may support the advertising of a number of products. More positively, the Discoveries of Spain and Portugal have often been employed as a way of making products more immediately recognisable and appealing. The prime opportunity for adopting this strategy was provided by the World Fair events taking place in Spain in 1992 and in Portugal in 1998. Any advertisement referring directly or indirectly to the heroic feats of the past, whether through a visual image or even a canonical literary work, is believed to suggest positive values that may be manipulated for the purposes of marketing products or services, in Portugal or in other countries.

In an earlier study (Odber de Baubeta, 1996), I noted how 'multinational companies run a campaign in a particular country using text in the local language and reinforcing their message with an important cultural icon, specific to the society in which they are advertising', and singled out as illustrations of this process an advert for the Sony Hiblack Triniton television set that showed, on the screen of an actual television set, the

Padrão dos Descobrimentos (Monument to the Discoveries), as well as one for the international accounting firm Coopers & Lybrand (*Grande Reportagem*, 1992), which also had a photograph of the same Lisbon Monument, with the heading 'Uma Garantia de Êxito' (A Guarantee of Success).

The Banco Português do Atlântico adopted a similar procedure in one of their 1990s campaigns, making the most of the associations between their name and the noun 'conquista' (conquest or success). As a result, we find the ambiguous heading 'Participe da Conquista do Atlântico', which variously means 'Take part in the Atlantic's Success', 'Take part in the Conquest of the Atlantic', 'Take part in the Atlantic's Conquest'. The Discoveries discourse is reinforced by the use of 'pioneiro' (pioneer), 'vencedores' (conquerors, winners), and 'novos rumos' (new directions).

Seiko and the Age of Discovery (1992)

At the beginning of the 1990s, Seiko ran a global campaign ambiguously called *The Age of Discovery*, and which relied largely on images of sailing ships and allusions to past glories (Odber de Baubeta, 1995). In addition to television advertisements, Seiko published a series of print adverts which had been translated into different languages, including Portuguese, with such headings as 'O Tempo dos Descobrimentos', 'O Tempo das Descobertas' (translated in both cases as The Time of the Discoveries), 'A Marca do Tempo' (The Trademark/Mark of Time). In general terms, 'Descobrimentos' evokes the whole overseas endeavour, while 'descoberta' would normally refer to one specific instance, such as the discovery of Brazil or the sea route to India.

These advertisements are all variations on a theme. Seiko wish their product to be associated with the positive values of courage, adventurousness and modernity and therefore rely heavily on Discoveries discourse with lexical items such as 'aventuras' (adventures), 'novos caminhos' (new paths), 'fronteiras expandidas' (extended frontiers), 'conquista' (conquest), 'glória' (glory). This explanation is borne out by an article in the Portuguese *TV Guia Internacional* for October 1998, 'Quinhentos artistas comemoram a Descoberta' (Five hundred artists commemorate the Discovery), or rather the 500th anniversary of the discovery of Brazil:

> Os 500 anos da descoberta do Brasil estão a ser evocados com um grande festival cultural na cidade de S. Paulo.

> (The quincentenary of the discovery of Brazil is being evoked in a great cultural festival in the city of São Paulo.)

A Spanish example – Carabela Santa María Brandy

As was to be expected with the Expo and the Olympics, 1992 gave rise to a whole series of Discoveries-related advertisements in Spain. By way of an example, we find an advert for Carabela Santa María Brandy that occupies a double-page spread in parchment colour, imitating an old manuscript, with hand-written text, fragments of a map, illustrations of caravels, a coffee mill, coffee beans, a cup of coffee and the brandy itself. According to the text, the company, Osborne, wishes to thank America for its contribution to the world, and especially for coffee, which goes so well with Carabela brandy, even though coffee did not in fact originate in that continent. Given the extremely tenuous connection between the product being advertised and the Discoveries – the name of Columbus' ship – this advertisement was either written tongue-in-cheek or the copywriter was desperate to cash in on the 1992 celebrations in order to use such clichés as 'un nuevo mundo de sensaciones' (a new world of sensations).

The Portuguese Tourist Board (1994)

An advertisement was published by the Portuguese Tourist Board in 1994 as part of an on-going series in the English quality press, and was presumably aimed at the kind of middle-aged, middle-class British consumers who look for 'cultural experiences' rather than mere sun, sea and sand. The photograph, taken from the Tagus River, shows Henry the Navigator, the leading figure in the *Padrão dos Descobrimentos* statue, with the Torre de Belém in the background, at sunset, silhouetted against a darkly golden sky. The text, written in a fairly conversational register, addressing its readers directly, explains the significance of the image:

> Many old folk have stories to tell. Like this 600-year-old Portuguese.
>
> You're looking at Henry the Navigator. But don't be fooled by appearances. This year is the young Prince's 600th birthday.
>
> As you'd expect from someone of this great age he has one or two experiences to relate. He founded the Sagres School by gathering sailors, cartographers and astronomers and taught the world how to navigate. He organized the first maritime European expeditions to Africa and populated many territories. And he inspired the Portuguese Vasco da Gama to plot a nautical route to India, Pedro Álvares Cabral to reach Brazil and Fernão de Magalhães to make the first circumnavigation of the world.
>
> Not surprisingly, the influence of our most famous senior citizen is noticeable in many countries.
>
> From Japan, where Portuguese words form part of the language, to the United States where the statue of Cabrilho stands as a memento of his arrival in California, to South Africa, where a monument was raised to commemorate the rounding of the Cape of Good Hope.
>
> If Portugal had such a role in linking together so many cultures, the credit goes to such men as Henry the Navigator.
>
> The thrill of discovery. Portugal.

This advertisement is notable for what it does not say, about Henry's questionable conduct of fifteenth-century Portuguese politics, his shared responsibility for the futile death of his brother, the Infante Santo D. Fernando, the wars with Spain, and, in respect of the Discoveries, the shipwrecks, slavery and unabashed human greed that marked the entire process. But these facts do not sit comfortably with the soft sell of the tourist ad, and there are limits to how much history the average holidaymaker wishes to absorb. The advert with its list of people and places is aimed at British people of a particular generation who learned history in this way – by rote – at school. The slogan, 'The thrill of discovery', which continues to appear in Portuguese Tourist Board advertisements, functions on at least two different levels, as both an incitement and a promise to those intrepid travellers willing to explore Portugal, Madeira and the Azores, and as a reminder of Portugal's glorious past.

Banco de Portugal (Expresso, 1990s)

The Banco de Portugal also avails itself of the Discoveries motif, in an informative advertisement for their new banknotes:

> Todas as novas notas contam a Epopeia dos Descobrimentos.
> Conheça agora mais duas páginas da nossa História.

> Mais duas ilustres personagens dos Descobrimentos voltam a figurar nas nossas notas. Pedro Álvares Cabral na nota de 1000 escudos. Uma nota bonita, de elementos acastanhados na frente, onde se destaca a efigie do navegador, impressa a violeta. No verso, uma caravel quinhentista e toda uma profusão de cores e temas tropicais que celebram a descoberta do Brasil.
> Na nova nota de 10.000, temos o Infante D. Henrique, que tanto fez pelos Descobrimentos, que ficou com o cognome de 'O Navegador'. Traz como elemento de segurança um leão que muda de cor, segundo o ângulo de visão. No verso, pode-se ler um excerto do poema de Fernando Pessoa, 'Deus quer, o Homem sonha, a Obra nasce…'

> (All the new notes recount the Epic of the Discoveries.
> Now learn two more pages in our History.

> Two more illustrious characters of the Discoveries return to figure on our notes. Pedro Álvares Cabral on the 1,000 escudo note. A pretty note, with brown elements at the front, from which stands out the effigy of the navigator, printed in purple. On the back, a fifteenth-century caravel and a profusion of colours and tropical themes that celebrate the discovery of Brazil.
> On the new 10,000 escudo note, we have Prince Henry, who did so much for the Discoveries that he was given the nickname of 'The Navigator'. For security it has a lion that changes colour, according to the angle of vision. On the back, one can read an extract from the poem by Fernando Pessoa, 'God wishes, Man dreams, the Work is born…')

Issued by Portugal's most important financial institution, the notes have been designed to reflect national pride in the Discoveries, incorporating an oblique allusion to Luís de Camões, Portugal's National Poet and author of the epic poem *Os Lusíadas*. Like his distinguished predecessor, Fernando Pessoa celebrated the Portuguese maritime undertaking, in *Mensagem*, from which the quotation is taken. What is interesting is the fact that the copywriter felt it necessary to remind the general Portuguese public who these figures are and why they should be remembered.

DHL (Expresso, 1990s)

In the previous advertisement, we saw an instance of a particularly popular advertising gambit, the use of a quotation from a famous literary figure. DHL modify this technique in an ad for their courier services, simultaneously misquoting and updating a much cited line from Camões' *Os Lusíadas*. The original line reads: 'Por mares nunca d'antes navegados' (Through previously uncharted seas), giving, instead, 'Por terras, ar e mares nunca dantes...' (Through lands, air and seas never before...).

Soporcel (Expresso, 1990s)

Soporcel have also made use of national icons, naming their photocopying paper 'Navigator', using the cartoon image of a ship on the high seas and a man in renaissance costume at a ship's wheel, along with wordplays such as:

> O papel padrão dos Portugueses.
> Navigator assinala a Grande Descoberta: o papel para fotocópia mais avançado do mercado.
> Navigator – a marca das grandes descobertas no papel mais avançado do mundo.

> (The standard paper for the Portuguese/The paper that sets the standard for the Portuguese.
> Navigator points to the Great Discovery: the most advanced photocopying paper in the market.
> Navigator – the trademark/watermark of great discoveries on the most advanced paper in the world.)

'O papel padrão dos Portugueses' is certainly an effective slogan. It echoes the prestigious *Padrão dos Descobrimentos* (Monument to the Discoveries) and links the product closely to the national identity. There is a strong suggestion that this photocopying paper sets the standard by which all other brands of paper will be judged, and has become the norm for the consumer. The advertisement also hints that the Portuguese technical expertise that made the Discoveries possible is now being applied to the manufacture of office supplies. In any event, the copywriter has created an association between this company, the notion of progress, and the Portuguese people.

Rall Office Furniture (Expresso, June 1998)

Rall, suppliers of office furniture, use a suggestive, modern design that resembles a caravel, followed by the legend 'Viagem para a descoberta' (Journey towards the discovery). This might in fact be the Portuguese title of a Jules Verne novel, with all its connotations of derring-do. The link between image and text is achieved through the lexical items 'ousadia' (boldness), 'recompensas' (rewards), 'sonhar' (to dream), and most explicitly, the verb 'descobrir'. We also note that the copywriter has embedded a proverbial saying in the text. 'Por vezes, a ousadia tem recompensas como estas' (At times, audaciousness has rewards like these), which echoes such sayings as 'Fortune favours the bold'.

Míele Electrical Appliances (Máxima, 1995)

In this ad, Míele talk about 'o espírito da descoberta' (the spirit of discovery) in relation to their electrical appliances. In a double-page spread, the left-hand page tells that in 1970, there were still discoverers in Portugal, those clients who bought their machines. The right-hand page tells us that the spirit of discovery is not always risky, since many Míele customers – described as pioneers – are still using the appliances they bought twenty-five years ago.

Absolut Vodka (Expresso, 1998)

The Portuguese ad for the Swedish vodka Absolut, reissued in 1998 to coincide with EXPO '98, bears the legend ABSOLUT LISBON. Set against a quintessentially Portuguese background of traditional blue tiles with a maritime motif, we see a ship in the vodka bottle. Not just any ship but a traditional Portuguese caravel. And underneath, the ambiguous recommendation, in English: 'Enjoy the treasures of the oceans at EXPO' 98 in Lisbon'.

Magellan clothing (1999)

This brand is mentioned in the Pseud's Corner section of the satirical review, *Private Eye* (20 August 1999, p. 13), presumably because the advertising puff contained on the clothing label is deemed to be excessively pretentious. There is no indication as to where the product originates, but the link between the brand name and the discoveries stereotype is certainly present:

> Ferdinand Magellan's 1519 expedition was man's first successful circumnavigation of the globe and one of the most important journey's [sic] ever undertaken, leading man out of the dark ages. And so it is with Magellan clothing. Quality and style that break through the myth of expensive prices for designer labels; and instead, bring to you classic, value clothing with a touch of adventure.

Casa do Azeite (Expresso, January 2000)

In January 2000, a new advertising campaign was reviewed in the Portuguese quality press:

> Azeite português à conquista do Brasil

> (Portuguese oil conquering/winning over Brazil)

According to the article, Portuguese olive oil producers have launched an advertising campaign to implant Portuguese olive oil in the Brazilian market. Their campaign takes as a main theme the discovery of Brazil by the Portuguese, and makes use of headlines such as:

> Um dos primeiros portugueses a desembarcar no Brasil. E até hoje um dos mais queridos

> (One of the first Portuguese to set foot in Brazil. And one of the best loved to this very day)

A terra ainda nem era redonda e os portugueses já faziam o melhor azeite do mundo

(The earth wasn't even round and the Portuguese were already making the best oil in the world.)

The campaign strategy is quite clear. The Portuguese are playing on their historical relationship with Brazil, taking advantage of the anniversary celebrations, in order to compete more aggressively against Argentina and Spain. There is no hint in the article that this approach is politically incorrect or inappropriate.

The Empire fights back (*Veja*, 1990s)
In an interesting reversal of the discoveries topos, a Brazilian advert for Stern shows a photograph of items of gold jewellery in the shape of feathers, and has a wordplay on the verb 'conquistar' (to conquer). Feathers are frequently associated with indigenous peoples, who use(d) them as objects of adornment. In case readers do not make this association, the text explains the image:

Viu por que os conquistadores acabaram conquistados?

(Have you seen why the conquerors ended up being conquered?)

The advertisement fits stereotypical notions of the 'other', fostered by the Romantic literature of Alencar in Brazil (compare with J. Fenimore Cooper or Chateaubriand for North America), whereby the 'acceptable' national ancestor is an Indian rather than an African. Thus Indian art is a suitable object of desire, in much the same way as the beautiful Indian maiden (Iracema, or even Pocahontas), is the object of desire of the European colonising male.

Conclusions
Although we have only considered a limited selection of advertisements, it is clear that there are no restrictions on those products or services that can be marketed using the Discoveries icons, the technique being equally applicable to office equipment or the entire country of Portugal. The Portuguese Discoveries, symbolised in stone by the *Padrão dos Descobrimentos*, lauded in the verses of Camões and Pessoa, printed on banknotes, remain the ultimate symbol of Portuguese national identity and achievement, and one which advertisers are only too happy to exploit.

As regards the vocabulary used in these advertisements, the range is not especially wide and collocations do not seem to vary greatly. The most cursory survey reveals that a small core of lexical items is used repeatedly, sometimes on their own, sometimes locked into binary oppositions such as past/present, present/future, Old World/New World, backward/forward. It seems that selected words associated with the Discoveries have been appropriated by the copywriters because they satisfy their needs, in just the same way as advertisers habitually draw on the Old and New Testaments, proverbs and literary fairy tales, in order to transmit their messages.

This constant referring to an epoch of global achievement does not signify a desire to (re)conquer the world. If we pause to reflect on the binary oppositions, it becomes clear that the past is mentioned as a counterpoint to technological progress already achieved and those advances to come in the future. Like the electronically generated icons we find at the top of our computer screens, the caravel and the *Padrão dos Descobrimentos* have become a rapid and effective means of attracting attention, ensuring instant recognition or identification, and allowing advertisers to express aspirations and desires.

If these advertising texts have been interpreted correctly, it seems that for reasons of national pride or nostalgia, the Portuguese still wish to be perceived as a race of people characterised as audacious, courageous and heroic. The Portuguese are by their very nature – or so the advertisers would have us believe – intrepid explorers, bold adventurers, and above all, successful. The Portuguese national identity, if we can talk about such a thing, is still bound up with the connotations generated by the Discoveries, dreams of fame and glory, the promise of rewards. For these reasons, the *Descobrimentos*, used, it must be said, as an extremely nebulous abstract concept rather than a set of concrete historical references to countries, conquests and abuses, have been used to sell Portuguese consumers not only a wristwatch or a washing machine, but more significantly, a globally positive image of themselves. Now, in the first year of the twenty-first century, it remains to be seen whether companies in Portugal will continue to tailor their campaigns to meet local tastes, expectations and cultural values, using timeless Portuguese cultural icons for promotional purposes.

References

Odber de Baubeta, P.A., 'Advertising Language in Translation: The Stylistics of Difference', *Donaire*, 5 (1995), pp. 47–53.

Odber de Baubeta, P.A., 'On Translating Advertisements' in Coulthard, M. &. Odber de Baubeta, P.A. (eds.), *Theoretical Issues and Practical Cases in Portuguese-English Translation*, Lewiston/Queenston/Lampeter: The Edwin Mellen Press, 1996, pp.157–80.

11 Whose Prize is it Anyway?
Press Coverage of the 1998 Nobel Prize-Winner for Literature

Sandi Michele de Oliveira
University of Copenhagen

On 8 October 1998, the Royal Swedish Academy announced the winner of the 1998 Nobel Prize for Literature: Portuguese novelist, José Saramago. It was, naturally, a personal triumph for the author, but it was also the first time the Nobel Prize for Literature had been awarded to an author writing in Portuguese. Further, it was only the fourth Nobel Prize awarded in any field to a Portuguese-speaker: in 1949 Egas Moniz won the Nobel for Medicine, and in 1996 D. Ximenes Belo and José Ramos-Horta (from East Timor) jointly won the Nobel Peace Prize, a fact alluded to by several newspapers, most clearly in *Jornal de Notícias*, in a full-page article entitled 'Quatro portugueses para três prémios Nobel' ('Four Portuguese for three Nobel Prizes'; JN, p. 50). Thus, the recognition assumed even greater significance, as some people hailed the award in the name of 'Portuguese Literature and the Portuguese language'. In fact, it was precisely because of the importance of the achievement and the small number of Nobel Prizes awarded to scholars in the Lusophone world, that the award naturally inspired a wave of patriotic pride. Detracting from the natural enthusiasm over the international acknowledgement of any Portuguese writer, however, is the controversy surrounding José Saramago regarding his political leanings, his religious persuasion and his literary style. As a result, there could be no straightforward association of the writer and his achievement with what many media and establishment figures seem to consider the main qualities and values of the national identity that Portugal should present to the world.

Saramago has been a staunch member of the Portuguese Communist Party since 1969, five years before the overthrow of the totalitarian regime in 1974. An atheist as well as a Communist, Saramago has never enjoyed favour with the Catholic Church in Portugal. His book *O Evangelho Segundo Jesus Cristo* (*The Gospel according to Jesus Christ*) was considered blasphemous by the Vatican (*Diário de Notícias*, p. 10), as Christ is presented as the son of a Roman soldier. In 1992, the Portuguese Government, responding to pressure from the Church, vetoed the nomination of this book for the European Award for Literature. In response to this act of censorship, Saramago moved in 1993 to Lanzarote, one of the Canary Islands. These two factors, combined with his literary style, which many readers find difficult, have made him an unpopular figure in both literary and social circles.

The Nobel Committee announced the Prize winners on 8 October 1998, and the first newspaper coverage appeared the following day. Nine newspapers available that evening in Évora were purchased for this study: *Diário de Notícias, Correio da Manhã, Jornal de Notícias, Record, Semanário, O Independente, 24 Horas, A Capital* and *Público*. It took only a glance at the front pages to confirm that the news coverage not only reported the controversy over Saramago but, in some cases, actually intensified it. Given the prestige of the Nobel Prize for Literature, on the one hand, and the equivocal status of Saramago, on the other, what is interesting is the manner in which the accolades are presented, and to whom they are directed. In this chapter we analyse front-page layouts, examining the coverage of Saramago in relation to the other news stories of the day. We consider the headlines and the particular focus of the stories on Saramago – his biography, his lifestyle, his religious and political affiliations, his writings – we compare individuals' reported reactions to the news and consider two cartoon strips which appeared in the newspapers. We conclude by describing the image of Saramago which emerges from the press coverage.

Front Page Coverage

Kress & van Leeuwen's (1998) critical analysis of front page coverage in newpapers serves as the reference point for the consideration of page layouts. Their analysis demonstrates that the information value and the salience of news stories both reflect and are shaped by specific layout strategies. They treat 'visual cues' as an indication of the degree of salience given to a particular story, and they describe several types of visual layouts:

a   a vertical page division, in order to contrast news stories which represent what is 'given' (left) and what is 'new' (right)
b   a horizontal page division, to compare the 'ideal' (top) with the 'real' (bottom)
c   a division between what is central and marginal
d   a triptychal layout, in which the central piece serves the function of 'mediator' of the two outer stories.

Each of the Portuguese newspapers analysed here uses either a horizontal or vertical division. The amount of first-page coverage given to Saramago ranges from one-tenth of a page (*O Independente*) to approximately nine-tenths (*Diário de Notícias*). In addition to the *Diário de Notícias*, three other papers carried a picture of Saramago covering half of the page or more (*Correio da Manhã*, *Público* and *Jornal de Notícias*). Indeed, every newspaper included a photograph of José Saramago on its front page, except *A Capital*, which opted instead for a picture of a Lisbon street showing a signpost carrying the message, *Parabéns, José Saramago* ('Congratulations, José Saramago').

Three papers have front-page layouts which are particularly striking: Nearly the entire front page of *Diário de Notícias* is devoted to Saramago, shown holding a ball up to his eye. The picture is in black and white, with the exception of the ball, which is golden. Saramago's signature is centred under the picture, and appears at the top of every page of the newspaper. This coverage, the greatest devoted to Saramago by any newspaper, demonstrates that it was judged to be the most important story of the day.

Record is a newspaper devoted to sport. On the cover, Saramago and Artur Jorge (a football coach taking charge of a French club) are encased in a full-colour image of the

Portuguese flag, thus linking their individual achievement to the glory of the nation. Above the picture are the words: 'Valores portugueses triunfam no mundo da cultura e do desporto: VENCEDORES' (Portuguese values triumph in the world of culture and of sport: WINNERS). Using Kress & van Leeuwen's model, we see that the preferential treatment is given to Artur Jorge, whose picture appears on the right, in the space reserved for what is 'new'. Additionally, the picture of Artur Jorge is slightly larger than that of Saramago and, more importantly, he appears to be gazing at the reader, while Saramago is looking to the sideways and down, as if he were avoiding eye contact.

The newspaper *24 Horas* has a tabloid style. There are three pictures on the front page, with both a horizontal and a vertical division. At the top right of the page, is a small picture of Artur Jorge, with the accompanying quotation: 'Estou feliz!' ('I'm happy!'). Below that Saramago shares principal billing with a story about strippers who have come from abroad to work in Lisbon. Saramago is shown at the left – in the 'given' space – in a vertical strip equivalent to a quarter of the remaining space on the page. There is a small picture of him, with his hands up at his chest, pointing inward, while at the right, occupying the remaining three quarters of the page, is a large picture of five strippers in various poses, some topless. One of the topless girls is cupping her breasts, providing a visual counterpoint to the picture of Saramago. The caption above the picture is: 'Elas aquecem as noites de Lisboa' (They heat up the Lisbon nights), and under the picture, which is about six times as big as that of Saramago, and in a very large typeface we read: 'Nuas para arrasar!' (stunning nudes!) with additional information in large, bold print.

There is a caption above Saramago's picture, presented within quotation marks: "O prémio é nosso, o dinheiro é meu…" (The prize is ours, the money is mine), so we are led to believe these were his exact words. Our first impression of Saramago is a negative one – that he cares only about the prize money, and is crass enough to say so. The impression given compares unfavorably with his treatment in *Público*, which shows him kissing a woman's hand (p. 2), with the caption: 'Se me permitem, embora o prémio seja de todos, já que estamos nisto, eu fico com o dinheiro' (If you please, while the prize may be for all, now that we are on the subject, I will keep the money). This is more likely to be an exact quotation, given its style and length. It seems likely that Saramago's remark been selectively edited by *24 Horas*, perhaps merely to achieve brevity, since the information provided below the picture is more balanced: Saramago dedicates his prize to his readers and to the Portuguese language; Saramago says, good-humouredly, that the money will remain with him; all of Portugal salutes him; and, the bishops have a bitter pill to swallow.

In each of the daily newspapers, the photograph of Saramago appears on the left. The only paper to feature Saramago on the right is *Semanário*, a weekly paper which happens to be published on Fridays. In this case, the picture is located below the fold, which places it in the quadrant which Kress & van Leeuwen describe as 'real' and 'new'. Interestingly, the picture of Saramago fills more than one-quarter of the page, and this story constitutes the only good news of the week. The other stories relate to corruption, political conflicts, counterfeit stock certificates, and a call by the Social Democrat Party for State funding of election campaigns.

Headlines

The overall coverage of Saramago in these publications reveals some interesting features, as there is great variation in the length and the type of coverage. Through an analysis of the headlines and the layout of the articles, we will argue that much less attention is paid to the accomplishments of the man than to the importance of the prize for Portugal. For example, *Diário de Notícias,* which has the largest number of pages and articles devoted to various aspects of the Saramago story, does not congratulate him as the individual who won the Prize in its main coverage. Rather, the newspaper focuses on the fact that in 1998 Portugal was the centre of international attention in several contexts: Expo '98 in Lisbon, Portugal's inclusion as a 'founding member' of the Euro, the Ibero-American Summit in Porto (and that city's nomination as the European Capital of Culture for the year 2001) and the opening of one of Europe's longest bridges (Ponte Vasco da Gama). Winning a Nobel Prize was just the icing on the cake. None of these events is ascribed to the accomplishments and work of a single person; thus, by describing the Portuguese language and Portuguese literature as the winners of the Nobel Prize the newspaper depersonalises the award, placing it in the category of collective achievements.

The stories in *Diário de Notícias* focus on the pride felt by Saramago's wife, daughter and publisher, yet no direct statement of pride in Saramago is to be found in the ten pages of articles. We find congratulations mentioned twice: first, 'Atenção, lisboetas, somo campeões do mundo de Literatura!' (Attention, Lisbonites, we are the world champions of literature!; p. 7) and second, 'Comunistas felicitam camarada de partido' (Communists congratulate party comrade; p. 8). All in all, one might assume that Saramago deserves praise from his family, publisher and comrades (but not necessarily from 'us', while 'we' [Lisbonites, and other readers] congratulate ourselves as winners).

Included in *Diário de Notícias,* however, is a literary supplement *JornaLivros,* printed in Portugal, but registered in Mexico City. Its sponsorship includes UNESCO and the Inter-American Development Bank, and it is furnished free with twenty-five newspapers in Ibero-American nations. It is, therefore, not exclusively a Portuguese publication. At the back of the supplement, on the last two-page spread, is a picture of Saramago that spans nearly a page-and-a-half. To the right, written by hand and signed by the newspaper's director, Mário Bettencourt Resendes, is the following: 'O Diário de Notícias felicita José Saramago, Prémio Nobel de Literatura de 1998' (The *Diário de Notícias* congratulates José Saramago, 1998 Nobel Prize-Winner for Literature). This, the most explicit statement of congratulations extended to Saramago by any newspaper, does not appear, we should note, in its regular pages. Nevertheless, the amount of overall coverage, the inclusion of Saramago's signature on every page of the newspaper, and this congratulatory statement in the literary supplement demonstrate that *Diário de Notícias* gives the greatest support to Saramago.

In contrast, the headlines in *A Capital* seem to suggest that Saramago was not the best choice. There is a two-page centrefold spread entitled, 'Não nasci para isto' (I wasn't born for this; p. 20–9), which could be interpreted as Saramago's own feeling that he is not an appropriate choice for the award. A half-page article is entitled, 'Ele está sempre a ganhar Nóbeis' (He is always winning Nobels – a comment from a university student in Lisbon heading an article on the difficulty that university students have in understanding his literary style, (p. 31). Another headline, 'O prémio para um "comunista inveterado"' (A prize for an 'inveterate Communist'), introduces an article in which criticisms of the Catholic Church (both in Portugal and in the Vatican) are presented.

In *Público* several headlines focus more on aspects of Saramago's humanity than on the award itself. For example, he broke into tears upon hearing the news: 'E Saramago chorou' (And Saramago cried), (p. 2); he was in the Frankfurt Airport when the news broke: 'A bagagem do viajante' (The luggage of the traveller) (p. 3); and he maintains his membership in the Communist Party despite overall membership figures having declined in recent years: 'Ser escritor comunista, hoje' (Being a Communist writer today) (p. 3). The newspaper also relates how he became an author and the story of an inter-family quarrel which led to Saramago's family leaving his birthplace in 1924: 'Catarinos contra Saramagos' (Catarinos versus Saramagos) (p. 9).

In *Record* only two pages (6–7) are devoted to Saramago. The headline of the major articles in the 'given' space on the left is: 'Vaticano critica escolha: "Entregaram prémio a um comunista"' (The Vatican criticises choice: 'They have given the prize to a Communist') and 'Saramago foi de tudo na vida: De serralheiro mecânico a escritor de sucesso' (Saramago has been everything in life: From machinist to successful writer). On the right-hand side of the page, there is a picture of Saramago at the top, under which the caption reads: 'José Saramago, qual "estrela" desportiva, aclamado na feira do livro de Frankfurt. Afinal recebeu o Prémio Nobel' (José Saramago, like a sports 'star', acclaimed at the Book Fair in Frankfurt. Finally he has received the Nobel Prize) (p. 6). Underneath the picture is an article headlined 'Nobel da Literatura 1998 ganho por José Saramago' (Nobel for Literature 1998 won by José Saramago). At the bottom of the page is an article on the four Nobel Prizes awarded to Portuguese-speaking people.

On the facing page, the largest headline is at the top: 'Portugal de novo na moda; o que é pequeno é bonito' (Portugal once again in fashion – small is beautiful), which appears just below a smaller heading: 'Prémio Nobel de José Saramago marca ano de sucesso para o País' (Nobel Prize of José Saramago marks a year of success for the Nation) (p. 7). Underneath this article, which fills approximately half a page, are the reactions of individuals, which will be considered below. A column to the right, approximately one-seventh of the width of the page, carries an article declaring this a news item the size of the world: 'Uma notícia do tamanho do mundo'. Nevertheless, given its small size relative to the other articles on the two-page spread, it seems insignificant. The three major articles form a triptych. The article declaring Saramago the winner of the 1998 Nobel Prize for Literature serves as an obvious mediator between the Vatican's disapproval of a Communist winning the award, on the left, and the amount of media attention Portugal has received throughout the year on the right. Perhaps surprisingly, the coverage in these two pages is balanced: while the controversy is mentioned, the news stories focus objectively on Saramago's life, his works, the debate on his merits as a Nobel recipient, and his place among the other lusophone Nobel winners. However, with an average daily circulation of approximately 140,000, nearly twice that of *Diário de Notícias* or *Público* and no particular political agenda, the objectivity of *Record* is logical from a marketing point of view.

Individual Reactions

The individual reactions of political, literary and religious figures are included in several of the papers. The framing of the comments – both in terms of their visual presentation in the newspapers and the way they are introduced – is illuminating. The first issue is that of the different presentations of the reactions (see Table 1)

The controversy regarding Saramago is reflected in the labels some of the newspapers have chosen for the section on reactions, and newspapers previously identified as providing coverage which is balanced (*Diário de Notícias, Record* and *Público*) continue this policy on these pages. Space does not permit a complete analysis of the reactions expressed; nevertheless, the following table summarises the comments, presented in a selection of the newspapers, of those asked for their reaction(see Table 2).

With the exception of *Jornal de Notícias*, praise for Saramago is provided either exclusively or prior to other comments in more than half of the commentaries published in each newspaper, but significant numbers of respondents choose to focus on the honour accruing to Portuguese literature or the Portuguese language.

Sincere and whole-hearted congratulations to Saramago can be seen in the reaction of Rui Alarcão, although even he refers first to the honour the award means for Portuguese literature:

> Finalmente foi feita justiça à literatura portuguesa. E, premiando José Saramago, que é realmente um dos nomes maiores dessa mesma literatura, em meu entender, a escolha não podia ser melhor.   (*DN*, p. 3).

Newspaper	Heading of the Section on Reactions to the News
24 Horas	*O que eles disseram* (What they said)
A Capital	*Palmas, vénias, louvores e insultos à mistura* (Applause, bows, praise and insults mixed together)
Correio da Manhã	*Todos os nomes … 'Mas'…* (All the names… 'But'…)
Diário de Notícias	*Ganhou a língua e toda a literatura portuguesa* (Portuguese language and literature won)
O Independente	*Amores e ódios* (Loves and hates)
Jornal de Notícias	*Palavras soltas* (Isolated words)
Público	*Reacções* (Reactions)
Record	*Reacções à decisão da Academia* (Reactions to the decision of the Academy)
Semanário	*As reacções possíveis* (Possible reactions)

Table 1

Individual Reactions to the News					
	Diário de Notícias	*O Público*	*24 Horas*	*Jornal de Notícias*	*Record*
Congratulating Saramago primarily	4	17	6	5	5
Congratulating Portuguese Literature or Portuguese Language primarily	1	11	4	4	2
Stating the selection of Saramago was unfortunate		1		1	
Other		6	3	7	1
TOTAL	5	35	13	17	8

Table 2

(Finally justice has been done to Portuguese literature. And, in awarding the prize to José Saramago, who is truly one of the greats of that same literature, in my understanding, the choice could not have been better.)

On the other hand, one of the clearly negative reactions, also in *Diário de Notícias*, was from D. Duarte Pio (who would have a claim on the Portuguese throne, if Portugal reverted to a monarchy). His comments sound surprisingly disparaging:

É um autor de leitura difícil e pesada, que insulta abertamente os sentimentos cristãos. Duvido que os membros do júri tenham lido os seus livros. É como se tivéssemos ganho o campeonato de futebol. É bom mas não tem muito conteúdo. (*DN*, p. 6).

(He is an author whose work is difficult and turgid, who openly insults Christian sentiments. I doubt that the members of the jury have read his books. It is as though we had won a football championship. It is good, but it does not mean much.)

On the other hand, the statement printed in *O Independente* is fuller, and his views are more balanced:

Por um lado, como português, fico satisfeito que a língua portuguesa seja reconhecida internacionalmente deste modo. Mas estou convencido que há outros escritores da língua portuguesa, em Portugal e no Brasil, que são certamente muito melhores, mais interessantes, mais legíveis que o Saramago. E sobretudo não nos podemos esquecer que ele insultou várias vezes os sentimentos de muita gente, nomeadamente de todos os cristãos, por exemplo, ao escrever que Cristo é fruto de uma relação de Nossa Senhora com um soldado romano e outras barbaridades do género. E, portanto é uma pessoa que além de escrever num estilo difícil é um insulto a toda a cristandade e a milhões de pessoas no mundo. Por isso é que eu tenho pena que tenha sido exactamente uma pessoa tão polémica a ser escolhida. (*O Independente*, p. 17).

(On the one hand, I am happy that the Portuguese language has been recognised internationally in this fashion. However, I am convinced that there are other authors in Portuguese, in Portugal and in Brazil, who are certainly much better, more interesting, and more decipherable than Saramago. And, moreover, we must not forget that he has insulted many times the sentiments of many people, namely of all Christians, for example, in writing that Christ was the product of a relationship between the Virgin Mary and a Roman soldier, and other atrocities. Thus, in addition to being a writer with a difficult style, he is an insult to all of Christianity and to millions of people around the world. For that reason I am sorry that it was precisely such a controversial person who was chosen.)

The issue over which Saramago left Portugal to live in the Canary Islands – the removal of his name from the list of candidates for the European Literary Prize of 1992 – was instigated by the then Sub-Secretary of Culture António Sousa Lara. While the reactions of most people consulted are not always identical from paper to paper, they are similar enough for us to sense that the quotes are parts of a single longer response. The divergence in quotations for Sousa Lara, however, suggest that perhaps he was questioned at different times; four versions are compared (*Semanário, Diário de Notícias, Público,* and *O Independente*):

Aquilo que fiz na altura foi convicto de que estava a fazer o que devia. Fá-lo-ia na mesma, mesmo se soubesse que ele ia receber o Nobel. Isto não tem nada a ver com a estética, tem a ver com convicções. (*Semanário*, p. 6)

(At the time, I was convinced that I was doing what was right. I would do it again, even if I knew that he was going to receive the Nobel Prize. This has nothing to do with aesthetics, but principles.)

Sousa Lara congratulates himself for having principles but, ironically, neither recognises nor appreciates the same quality in Saramago. In *Diário de Notícias*, the comment is quite different:

Se hoje se mantivessem as mesmas circunstâncias, designadamente o regulamento do prémio e a obra em causa, tomaria a mesma decisão [de vetar *O Evangelho segundo Jesus Cristo* para o Prémio Europeu de Literatura]. Mas como político tenho uma característica, o fair play, e dou os parabéns ao vitorioso. (*DN*, p. 6)

(If today the same circumstances were in force, specifically vetting the award and the literary work in question, I would make the same decision [to veto...]. But as a politician I have a characteristic sense of fair play, and so I congratulate the victor.)

Again Sousa Lara congratulates himself, this time for 'fair play', rather than moral rectitude, as if he and Saramago were in direct competition. In his final comment he concedes defeat to the victor, suggesting that perhaps Saramago won by not playing fair. This viewpoint is stated more clearly in *Público*, in which Sousa Lara pompously claims Saramago had the advantage of a strong lobby (p. 8).

O Independente prints the longest statement by Sousa Lara, some 250 words. He starts by saying, 'Whether from a sense of "fair play" or patriotism, I take pride in the fact that the Nobel Prize for Literature was awarded to a Portuguese writer.' He then proclaims the decadence of Portugal and his feeling that the country is no more than a region of Spain, before returning to Saramago whose style and choice of topics he does not like. He continues at length on his own personal indifference towards great literature, claiming he is indifferent as to whether a book has depths to explore or not! There is a contradiction here: on the one hand, Sousa Lara takes pride in Portugal having received the Nobel Prize, but on the other he admits he neither knows nor cares about the subtleties and depth of the type of literature which is recognised by the Nobel Committee.

Comic Strips

There are few political cartoonists in Portugal, and only two newspapers have daily comic strips. Diário de Notícias carries a strip entitled 'Cravo e Ferradura', by Bandeira, and 'Público' carries 'Bartoon', by Luís Afonso. In the 9 October 1998 newspapers, both strips refer to the Nobel Prize, but in neither case is Saramago congratulated for his success. In 'Cravo e Ferradura' (DN, p. 2) the focus is on the cartoon characters, representing the Portuguese people, rather than on Saramago:

A: Saramago é Novel da Literatura! (Saramago is the Nobel in Literature)
B: Porquê tanto barulho? Tu não lês livros. (Why so much fuss? You don't read books.)
A: Sim, mas lá no estrangeiro vão pensar que leio. (Yes, but abroad they will think that I do.)

In 'Bartoon' (*Público,* p. 10), a bartender is talking to two cows, who are standing at the bar. There are four pictures, with one sentence each:

Entrámos no euro. (We entered the Euro.)
Realizámos a Expo. (We put on Expo.)
Ganhámos o Nobel da Literatura. (We won the Nobel Prize for Literature.)
Só vocês é que nos fazem passar vergonhas... ('Only you put us to shame...')

As with 'Cravo e Ferradura', the focus is on Portugal; here the implication is that the Nobel is just part of the country's overall success. While there is recognition of the importance of the Nobel Prize, no congratulations are given to Saramago; in fact, he is not even mentioned by name. Instead, his literary success is equated with the economic success of the country (which enabled it to enter the Euro in the first round) and with the tourist success of the Expo. Moreover, the cartoon focuses on 'Mad Cow Disease', a health problem not yet under control in Portugal in 1998, rather than Saramago, the major newsmaker of that day.

This examination of the press coverage has revealed that the award of the Nobel Prize to Saramago is presented as a national triumph for Portugal. Nevertheless, it is not the case that Saramago, the man, or even Saramago, the writer, is universally praised for his achievements. The controversy surrounding him is as alive as ever, and his identity as Nobel winner remains elusive. The subtitle for this chapter is 'Whose Prize Is it, Anyway?' This is a question raised in only one newspaper, *O Independente*, which presents coverage that is modest (two pages) but seems to step back from the fray and view the entire process more objectively. In fact, this newspaper was not originally included in the analysis, as its coverage of Saramago is so sparse. Even the front page coverage is misleading, for the only reference to the event is a small picture of Saramago and the word 'FINALMENTE!' (At last!) in letters less than three centimetres high. It is significant, however, that the main article in this newspaper, by Paula Moura Pinheiro, is entitled, 'O Nobel é nosso ou é dele?' (Is the Nobel ours or his?) (p. 17), with a smaller headline just above the text of the article: 'Depois de anos de conspirações frustradas e de expectativas goradas, o Nobel veio para um escritor português. É a felicidade nacional. De repente, todos estamos de parabéns!' (After years of frustrated conspiracies and of slashed expectations, the Nobel came to a Portuguese writer. This results in national happiness. Suddenly, all of us are to be congratulated!). The irony implicit in the headline becomes clear upon reading the article, as Pinheiro describes two aspects of Portuguese culture: nationalism and the depersonalisation of individual achievement.

The nationalistic response is demonstrated by the actions of those in Frankfurt Airport who persuaded Saramago to return to the Book Fair in Frankfurt, where Portuguese journalists were on hand, rather than fly to Spain. If he had not turned back, his first interview would have been in Madrid, drawing the attention of the international press to his isolation from daily life in his native country.

The depersonalisation of Saramago's individual achievement and the public's desire to bask in reflected glory is a separate issue. Pinheiro writes that Portugal's politicians wish to 'esticar o feliz evento como se fosse um mega-guarda-chuva onde todos nos podemos abrigar por instantes.' (stretch out the happy event, as though it were a mega-umbrella under which we could all take cover for a few moments) (*O Independente*, p. 17).

Implicit in both the issues raised is that the Nobel is 'ours'. Pinheiro concludes the article, however, by quoting António Mega Ferreira, an entrepreneur who is credited with giving Portugal a high profile in Europe and the world through the Frankfurt Book Fair and the Lisbon Expo,

> A vitória é exclusivamente de José Saramago. A vitória de um escritor é sempre um acto solitário. Acredito que Saramago está, neste momento, mais sozinho do que nunca. Que isto não é como a selecção de futebol (p. 17).

> (The victory is exclusively José Saramago's. The victory of a writer is always a solitary act. I believe that Saramago is, at this moment, more alone than ever. For this is not like the selection in football.)

This interpretation is mirrored and further substantiated in an editorial by Rui Zink, which appears just below Pinheiro's article, in the area Kress & van Leeuwen refer to as 'real'. The title of the editorial, 'The prize to the one who works for it', is an allusion to a slogan for agrarian reform, popular in the 1970s: 'The land to the ones who work it'. Zink states that while the prize may honour the entire country, the language and its literature, it was won specifically by Saramago:

> O prémio, o único realmente válido ao câmbio actual, honra uma língua e as literaturas que lhe dão uso. Mas o prémio a quem o trabalha, e quem o ganhou foi Saramago.

In this chapter we have seen how the real controversy regarding Saramago's personal and professional merits as a Nobel Prize winner have been presented and even shaped in the press. The analysis conducted of page layouts in newspapers demonstrates clearly the ambiguity of responses to this news event and the secondary position that Saramago, the man, is forced to occupy relative to the acclaim given to Saramago, as representative of the Portuguese nation, language and literature.

As do Kress & van Leeuwen, we also find that this is accomplished through a variety of means and to differing degrees in the various newspapers. No newspaper presents Saramago in an unfavourable light in its front-page presentation. However, the amount of coverage, the wording of the headlines of the news stories and the section on reactions, as well as the content included in the stories themselves, are designed to convey either praise or blame. These stories serve to diminish the importance of the award for the reader and, while they should be marginal, they occupy the central news space, in Kress & van Leeuwen's terms.

In considering the treatment of Saramago, however, we are forced to acknowledge the strange fact that, even at the time of his greatest triumph, he is neither undisputedly referred to as a great writer nor universally credited with having deserved the award. The analysis of the front-page layouts, headlines and article layouts and the comments of literary, political and religious figures provide confirmation of this. What overall picture emerges of Saramago, the man? We see an individual who, because of his convictions, has become very isolated from the society he writes about, so isolated that he no longer lives in his own country. Ironically, given his political leanings, Saramago seems to fit the description to Portugal herself that the former dictator, António Salazar, put forward on 18 February 1965: 'orgulhosamente só' (proudly alone). In winning the highest recognition possible in his field, Saramago's achievement curiously brings him the trappings of a national hero without quite making him one.

References

Kress, G. & van Leeuwen, T., 'Front Pages: (The Critical) Analysis of Newspaper Layout' in Bell, A. & Garrett, P. (eds.) *Approaches to Media Discourse,* Oxford: Blackwell, 1998, pp. 186–219.

Newspapers, all dated 9 October , 1998

24 Horas	*A Capital*	*Correio da Manhã (CM)*	*Diário de Notícias (DN)*
O Independente	*Jornal de Notícias (JN)*	*Record*	*Semanário.*

12 Nation and Nostalgia

The Place of Advertising in Popular Fictions

Nickianne Moody
Liverpool John Moores University

Popular expression during particular cultural periods can be characterised in terms of prevailing ideologies. During the 1980s and early 1990s in Britain the cultural climate was one of nostalgia, evident in the narrative discourse of *The Antiques Roadshow* (BBC1, 1979), *Brideshead Revisited* (Granada, 1981, repeated twice during the 1990s), *The Darling Buds of May* (Yorkshire, 1991–3), *Heartbeat* (Yorkshire, 1992–) and the rise in popularity of the National Trust. Televisual advertising in particular contributes to the cultural and textual practices of the period and is therefore a vital part of contemporary collective consciousness. Its imagery and structure are interconnected with popular fiction through tourism, identity, propositions of lifestyle, public discourse and the production of nostalgic narrative.

Although many sectors, for example bread, housing and holidays, promoted their products using nostalgic referents, it is the promotion of tea which best illustrates the discursive matrix active during this period. The direct association between fiction and tea advertising lies in the decision of manufacturing companies to sponsor specific drama programmes after the 1990 Broadcasting Act, for example, Tetley and *The Darling Buds of May* or Yorkshire Tea and *Heartbeat*. Tea and its connotations of a British national identity transcending class, regional and gendered experience becomes closely integrated with the popular fiction of a specific political period.

In a review of an exhibition at the National Gallery of Art in Washington in 1985, which was called *The Treasure Houses of Britain: 500 Years of Private Patronage and Collecting*, David Cannadine considered the cultural significance of staging such an event in the mid-1980s. The article is republished under the title 'Nostalgia' in his book *The Pleasures of the Past* (1989) and in it he identifies nostalgia as a recurrent cultural phenomenon. He distinguishes three distinct cultural climates of nostalgia, which have recurred during three economic depressions: the last quarter of the nineteenth century, the inter-war years and the post-1974 period. These periods of depression, although they do not repeat themselves exactly, do produce intense national interest in the past, which manifests itself in specific cultural forms and practices.

The common characteristics of these periods are: high unemployment, loss of overseas markets, complaints about both entrepreneurs and workers, renewed awareness of urban deprivation and the expression of popular unrest. The response to economic depression also engenders a shift to the political Right because divisions within the Left hinder effective opposition to Conservative government, as was the case for instance, with the governments of Salisbury, Baldwin and Thatcher. Recession, Cannadine argues, breeds reaction in Britain rather than revolution. Cannadine outlines cultural life at such times as withdrawn, escapist and discontented with contemporary society. Such a general mood results in the appeal of the rural and the cult of the country house.

Cannadine describes these periods as nostalgia booms. We can also regard many of the fictions recycled in our own period as a reduplication of nostalgia. For example, *Brideshead Revisited* is a nostalgic text which is itself nostalgic for the last quarter of the nineteenth century in a similar fashion to Agatha Christie's detective fiction. Their audiences in the 1980s and the 1990s, however, are nostalgic for the contemporary setting of this fiction, Cannadine's middle period of nostalgia, the apparently carefree hedonistic inter-war years which are represented to us as art decor interior, country house party and glamorous fashion. So texts from earlier periods are recycled because their nostalgia is culturally resonant. John Corner & Sylvia Harvey (1990) group these fictions in the category of heritage storytelling which they assert requires analytic attention to its various modes and imperatives and moreover, its various purposes, projections and assumptions. As we follow this fiction as it passes from the grand design of *Brideshead* into the comfortable nostalgia of *The Darling Buds of May* (screened during the Gulf War) we cannot overlook its relationship with tea advertising.

Rather than through a static statement, Tetley Tea's sponsorship was indicated through the insertion of animated sequences which introduced, commented upon and closed the episodes of *The Darling Buds of May*. The 'Tetley Tea Folk' were seated in their own living room, drinking tea and watching the same programme as the audience. Adopted as a promotional device by the company in the 1980s, the Tetley Tea Folk advertisements are structured by the ideological hierarchy of a family firm. Their work and family life portrayed in various advertising formats is emotionally rewarding but the adverts were screened when these two areas had become sources of national anxiety. In the same period, Yorkshire Tea was seen in association with *Heartbeat*, a police-centred detective series set in a rural community during the 1960s but broadcast at a point when the police were under severe media and public scrutiny for corruption and poor professional practice. In Britain, for example, the findings of Operation Jackpot were brought to trial starting a vociferous media debate about corruption and styles of policing. The two-year investigation into corruption in the Metropolitan Police was the most serious allegation against the force for twenty years. Misconduct concerning breaches of procedure in the trial and investigation of those suspected of killing Carl Bridgewater also became part of the debate in the British media at this time.

Although the quintessential nostalgia advertisement in Britain of this period is for bread, Yorkshire Tea also produced a series of television adverts in the early 1990s that capture the sense of nostalgia specific to this period. The 1973 campaign for Hovis was revised in 1993 to project the same nostalgic assertions of quality and value (Odber de Baubeta, in press). The mythology not only explores a valued past way of life but it negates an uncertain future. It does so through the acknowledgement of material possession and advancement of personal status within the contemporary period that can only be valued in relation to the past. For example the voice-over of a grandmother making tea recalls the warmth, affection and relative poverty of her childhood whilst acknowledging the material gain and security of her present. Her choice of tea is associated with the family values of the earlier, less affluent period without compromising working-class taste. The desired object of her youth, a special ornamental teapot, is in use today, thus confirming a sense of well-being on the part of the audience. Moreover, the anecdote she tells of her parents' love affirmed by extravagant gift giving is worthy of *The Antiques Roadshow*.

Typhoo Tea's print campaign from a slightly earlier period has a polysemic central picture of a letter or, as we learn, taste test report, with a cup of tea on a checked tablecloth (breakfast table) which is surrounded by a border of different ornamental teacups (*LIA*, 1998: 4). These range from the ordinary to the classic, representing different styles over eighty years which would be recognisable to the British reader through personal experience or antiques fairs and programmes. The narrative explanation of the statement, 'Every 4 weeks an 80-year-old reputation is put to the test' is one of enterprise:

> [...] John Sumner was a Birmingham grocer until, in 1905, for John opportunity knocked.
> His change of career (his tea break, perhaps?) was actually thanks to his sister.
> She had just tried a new kind of tea from Ceylon, with smaller leaf particles and a greater flavour than was usual in those teas.
> She liked it. She tried it on her gardener. He liked it too. It was, she declared a wonderful pick-me-up.
> 'John, why don't you sell this tea?' She suggested.
> And thus was the Typhoo Tea Company born. The rest, as they say is history [...]

This discussion contrasts with the Tetley Tea Folk commercials which take a paternal family firm as a given. Here the discussion between brother and sister leads to the founding of a company. By choosing this moment, nostalgia is focused not on past glory but on its anticipation. John Sumner's unnamed sister is an ordinary woman with good taste who prompts the founding of a household name.

The tenor of tea advertising stresses that tea is ordinary and its representation is very much concerned with quotidian lives. In contrast, the world of coffee drinking in Britain is advertised as exotic, educated, sophisticated, flirtatious, powerful or dangerous and erotic. The late 1980s is the period of the 'Gold Blend Couple' campaign for Nescafé whose romantic cliff-hangers were presented in the little-used form of serial advertising. It was so successful that the adverts became the basis for a novel (James, 1993). The promotion line for Kenco's instant coffee Carte Noire, 'un café nommé désir', with its portrayal of contemporary amorous couples in a print campaign during 1999 confirms the continuing distinction in Britain between paradigms of tea and coffee advertising.

However, British trends are reversed in Europe and this contrast is most apparent in advertising upmarket tea brands. Twinings promotes itself in France as 'The Tea' and heads its print campaign with the legends 'No Comment', 'No Compromise' and 'No

Sugar' (*LIA*, 1993: 5). The statements are produced in English and parody an earlier print campaign for the British newspaper *The Financial Times*. The words are accompanied by an off-centre, black and white photograph of individual men and women who represent the 'British' upper class, a status connoted by jewellery and expression. The claim made by their Norwegian campaign – 'Twinings Tea luxury everyday' – is also very significant for the 1980s. It comprises photographs of people drinking tea in a setting that in Britain is reserved for coffee, that is, outside the home (*LIA*, 1987: 6). The Tetley campaign in Sweden presents modern poetry (or a diary entry) where a person in the black and white crowd speculates on the life of colourful characters in the foreground. The external contemporary world and the association with youth and the extraordinary are features which once again in Britain would be applied to coffee or the innovation of herbal tea.

Another significant contrast between British and European tea advertising lies in different evocations of tea producing regions. In a print campaign for France, Twinings use a sensuous feminine evocation of the colonial period (*LIA*, 1999: 3). The legend 'Depuis 1706 l'eau a son parfum' introduces photographs of white women in oriental fabric or masculine colonial attire (pith helmet and white jacket). The images used are a pastiche of the style and manner of fashion photography and more specifically that of perfume advertising designed to give Earl Grey 'parfum d'averse', Golden Pekoe 'parfum d'orage' and Darjeeling 'parfum de mousson' teas a luxurious mystique. The connotations of a sensuous if not erotic ambience of colonial pleasure subvert the British adherence to tea advertising alluding to the wholesome functioning of Empire, one which fundamentally assumes a safe and secure past.

Therefore, in Britain, Twinings uses idealised colour drawings of Victorian social events to promote specific blends of tea, for example, Breakfast and Traditional Afternoon. In the 1990s, location-specific names for teas such as Darjeeling and Assam are realised by illustrations representing indigenous workers in these nineteenth-century colonial settings who are engaged in contented employment, for example shipping or picking tea, rather than the white middle-class consumer. Both depictions offer the everyday assurance of the business and ordered leisure of Empire, a style and set of imagery that is used by own brand blends of tea such as Somerfield.

The established order, comfort and normality of Empire is evoked in a different way, but to the same effect, by a 1987 Brooke Bond PG Tips campaign (*LIA*, 1987: 1). The aim is to affirm the quality, experience and leadership of the brand through the nostalgic use of images of childhood. The advert resembles the kind of general knowledge quiz to be found in pre-war children's books or magazines. The adverts ask, 'How many teas do you need to make a fine quality blend?' or 'At what speed would a tea bush grow to acquire the richest flavour?' Rather than 'interesting facts' the answers are presented as valuable, knowledge that has a use in education and the workplace. In answer to the first question, the 'child'/reader is presented with four non-white men in national costume. Their colonial origins are identifiable by the clues in small landscapes at their feet that contain regional architecture and, in two instances, animals as well. The men carry tea chests with a number on them followed by question marks from which the child should choose the right answer. The colourful drawings of the men contrast with the tea chests, which have been fashioned from tea leaves. In answer to the second question, four overseas animals are positioned at different entrances to a maze created from tea leaves. Despite its exotic and foreign origins, tea is invested with the assurance of tradition and ordinariness through the nostalgia of security associated with childhood learning.

Products at the lower end of the tea market also use associations with tradition and uncontested Victorian stability. The packaging for Rosie Lee tea bags is particularly interesting, since it contrasts the working-class connotations of the London slang name for the beverage with an image of Victorian middle-class propriety. (Rosie Lee is an example of Cockney rhyming slang, associated with the Cockney meaning of rosy as a favourable or a good omen; its use in this advertising as a nostalgic reference point belies its class purpose and origins). The *mise-en-scène* groups a handsome, wooden-framed black and white photograph of a Victorian couple in their respectable finery with a napkin in a silver ring. Tea is being poured into a china cup placed on a saucer with a silver spoon set on a lace tablecloth. Through the slogan 'Tea as it used to taste', it is given connotations of middle-class aspiration as a now affordable everyday consumable. Economy blended teas at the lowest end of the market also use the image of best china for the ritual of tea drinking.

Therefore the advert skilfully presents tea as respectable and common at the same time. This is the tea table of the aspirational working class which became part of the drive in the 1980s towards home ownership, escalating membership of the National Trust and notions of enterprise culture which underpin the fundamental changes in work practice, experience and policy that have taken place in Britain. In the popular imagination the ordinariness of tea in this advert is readily associated with the offer made by Typhoo Tea in 1996 to take a country house weekend or 'explore with English Heritage. Delve into the past and visit England's historic attractions with *two admissions for the price of one'*. Tea becomes part of the cultural practices of constructing national identity and historical narrative.

Altogether, tea advertising contributes to a very specific account of Empire and the past as a safe place, an account which becomes harder to challenge and dispel as it builds upon connotations of surety, success, family values, childhood, traditional authority and the notion of a golden age which has been matched if not surpassed. Frederick Jameson (1979) talks about the appeal of popular fiction as one of complicity. He considers popular fiction as able to manipulate people by providing pleasures which are complicit with an order based on domination and exploitation. Similarly, Roger Bromley (1978) has identified how money in romantic fiction comes to be detached from the realities of social relations and economy so that the signs of luxury, wealth and privilege can be readily enjoyed. The pleasures of the country house and the popular fiction of consumption in the 1980s in particular are those of ownership, material possession, security and confidence. During this period they have the connotations of luxury.

The literary critic Lionel Trilling (1967) sees the nineteenth century as a significant period for the understanding of pleasure. In his view, the growth of a luxury market in Britain, with its mass cultural appeal, enabled commodities to emerge and circulate as signs of pleasure. From this point, he argues, it is possible to observe 'the growing tendency of power to express itself mediatively, by signs and indices, rather than directly, by the exercise of force'. Within the new forms of social and economic organisation established during the nineteenth century, pleasure becomes a sign of power. It is these pleasures that are recycled within fiction and advertising during the 1980s and 1990s and that are promoted as legitimate and affordable. In the case of tea, its ordinariness becomes focused through nostalgia; the pleasures of consumption and the broader signs of luxury, a healthy well-fed family, material possessions, country houses and security, with which tea becomes associated, are mythologised as everyday expectations and available to all in Britain. This ideologically conditioned perspective contributed to support for and consent to government policies, as well as changes in social interaction and cultural practice.

The epitome of nostalgic advertising, emphasising a resilient British identity facing the possibility of chaos, is a short-lived television campaign for Typhoo Tea which was broadcast towards the end of *The Darling Buds of May* series in the early 1990s. The imagery combines distinctive red Typhoo Tea packaging and logo, with footage of the white cliffs of Dover and a speech from Shakespeare, more precisely John O'Gaunt's speech in Act II Sc. i of *Richard II*:

> This earth of majesty, this seat of Mars,
> This other Eden, demi-paradise,
> This fortress built by Nature of herself
> Against infection and the hand of war
> This happy breed of men, this little world
> This precious stone set in the silver sea,
> Which serves it in the office of a wall,
> Or as a moat defensive to a house,
> Against the envy of less happier lands,
> This blessed plot, this Earth, this realm, this England.

When this advert is considered in relation to Major's claims for a classless society and Englishness defined as warm beer and cricket matches of the sort recreated in Bates's novel then we find an instance of nostalgia which deviates from Cannadine's schema.

The crucial point about Bates' novel *The Darling Buds of May* is that it is not nostalgic. It satirises the post-war democratic settlement and changing social life in the 1940s and 1950s, particularly class experience which would result in the middle-class anxieties given full expression by the popular Ealing Comedies made for the cinema in the 1950s. The post-1974 period can be understood culturally as an ideological process of gaining popular consent to break the contract established by post-war policies for health, housing, welfare and nationalisation. Tea advertising and the television version of *The Darling Buds of May* in the 1990s are important texts both for the actual negotiation of that consent and also as a means to understand the nature of the hegemonic consensus.

Cannadine's choice of *Brideshead Revisited* as a nostalgic text celebrating the country house was actually written at the end of the Second World War. Waugh's novel was deeply nostalgic for the turn of the century and fearful of a democratic future. The novel was revised in 1957. The reason given for this in the new version's prologue was the author's sheer embarrassment at the excess of the novel's ornamental language, lavish descriptions of food and overall account of splendour which seemed rather distasteful to him in the post-war period. Since *The Darling Buds of May* was published in 1959, it is not inconceivable that the two were sold or borrowed from the library side by side. Waugh's villain, the cheerful scrounger Hooper, ready to thrive in the post-war economy, could easily be related to Bates's hero Pop Larkin, especially as hero and author are voicing a desire to tear down the inefficient country house and sell it for scrap to build up new housing for illegitimate children. The Larkin's family values are based on the gratification of material and physical needs. So although Bates uses the nostalgic staples of summertime and nature, his story is set in a forward-looking England of the 1950s. The Larkins are consumers, breaking with the austerity of their parents and surrounded by a mass of children who are indulged and can do whatever they want with their lives. Their consumer durables and experiences of nature are both there to be enjoyed in direct contrast to the local aristocracy who are down on their uppers and unable to survive in the new cultural and economic climate. This is an optimistic rather than wistful nostalgia. The Larkins are celebrations of 1950s' consumerism able to acquire the pleasures of upper-class luxury without the responsibility. Plenty is an element of nostalgia but it associates this pleasurable concept with the pain of Arcadia. The prospect of loss is a critical element present in nostalgia which is completely removed from its articulation in the 1980s and 1990s. The hint of Arcadia in the 1950s version of Bates' story which is effaced in the 1990s portrayal, is clear in the Shakespearean sonnet from which the book takes its title:

> Shall I compare thee to a summer's day?
> Thou art more lovely and more temperate.
> Rough winds do shake the darling buds of May
> And summer's lease hath all too short a date.

The changes between the televisual and the print fiction versions show how *The Darling Buds of May* has been recycled for the 1990s. The televisual text fills the screen with perpetual summer, the abundance of good food, disposable consumer durables, happy families, escapades, a 'loads-a-money' feel-good factor and a freedom of employment, a glorious nostalgia for the 1950s and early 1960s. In this fashion it can ignore the consequences of this lifestyle and override contemporary anxieties. Race, unemployment, the city and international relations are not an issue. Even the battle of the sexes is good humoured. It is this account of Merrie England with which tea manufacturers wish to associate themselves.

This is a land of plenty for the entrepreneur. Charley, the Larkins' prospective son-in-law, is being lured from his office job and secure pension to set up in his own business. Meanwhile Pop Larkin is taking over responsibility for the community from the upper-class feudal system without any need for the safety net of the welfare state.

The community will look after itself through the prosperity of its members. This last aspect is important if we consider it in the light of Brian Turner's (1987) view of nostalgia as a social and cultural discourse which expresses a particular kind of loss, that of personal wholeness and moral certainty. So nostalgic texts acknowledge the loss of individual freedom and the disappearance of genuine social relations. Central to the use of nostalgia is a concern with the perceived absence of meaningful social relationships and this is expressed, according to Turner in the representation of simplicity, personal authenticity and emotional spontaneity which is the essence of Pop Larkin and the discourses of tea advertising.

The perception of order conveyed by a mythology of Victorian stability becomes extremely attractive and culturally desirable. Therefore the garden which is the starting and closing point for each television episode is also another essential element of nostalgic imagery. Other nostalgic texts which work in a similar fashion such as Ellis Peter's *Cadfael* series from the 1980s realised on television in the 1990s and the *Miss Marple* (BBC1, 1984–92) television series of the same period make similar use of garden imagery.

In the face of questionable national identity, nostalgia is used to blur the recognition of contradictions. Nostalgia is therefore an acceptable mode that reconfigures the period between the end of the Second World War and the oil crisis in the mid-1970s for popular consumption as entertainment. It does so by presenting it as a period of individual enterprise resulting in the classless consumer. Criticism of the fantasy Britain that prevailed in popular media during the Thatcher era is commonly raised by cultural studies, particularly in relation to the heritage industry (Hewison, 1987). However, the argument that is being made here is that the ubiquity of the image of fantasy Britain is traceable from text to cultural practice in the advertising of tea and its account of ordinary Britain. The promotion of tea is instrumental in perpetuating a way of imagining Britain validated by a mythology of the imperial past and its benevolent continuity. The paradox or explanation of this mythology is that its retelling comes at the decisive end of many aspects of traditional forms of identity in terms of family, race and gender, the dismantling of nationalised industry and the welfare state. The stability of this imagery and its power to diffuse the recognition of a changing Britain meant that the England of tea advertising was the one turned to by the Conservative government to notify the public about the privatisation of water, power and transport utilities. Through this discursive matrix, Britain was offered the opportunity of prosperous change without the undesirable consequences of changing. The consensuality of the fiction and the discourse of which advertising is one part has been remarkable for its duration and hold over the popular imagination.

References

Lürzer's International Archive (LIA), 1 (1987), p. 29.
Lürzer's International Archive 6 (1987), p. 27
Lürzer's International Archive, 4 (1988), p. 36.
Lürzer's International Archive, 5 (1993), pp. 29–30
Lürzer's International Archive, 3 (1999), pp. 21–2

Bromley, R., 'Natural boundaries: the social function of popular fiction', *Red Letters*, 7 (1978), pp. 34–60.

Cannadine, D., 'Nostalgia' in *The Pleasures of the Past*, London: Collins, 1989, pp. 256–71.

Corner, J. & Harvey, S.,'Heritage in Britain: Designer History and the Popular Imagination', *Ten-8*, 36 (1990).

Hewison, R., *The Heritage Industry: Britain in a Climate of Decline*, London: Methuen, 1987.

James, S., *Love Over Gold*, London: Corgi, 1993.

Jameson, F., 'Reification and utopia in mass culture', *Social Text*, 1 (1979), pp. 130–48.

Odber de Baubeta, P.A., 'Bread, the Staff of Advertising', *Paremia*, Madrid: in press.

Trilling, L., *Beyond Culture*, Harmondsworth: Peregrine, 1967.

Turner, B.S., 'A Note on Nostalgia', *Theory Culture and Society*, 4 (1987), pp. 147–56.

13 Beyond the Modern and the Postmodern
European Soap Operas and their Adverts

Hugh O'Donnell
Glasgow Caledonian University

Introduction

This chapter is to some extent a spin-off from a much larger project in the course of which I analysed domestic soap-opera production in fourteen Western European countries in the 1990s (O'Donnell, 1999). These productions went out on both public service (psb) and commercial channels characterised by a wide variety of advertising regimes, ranging from no commercials at all (as in the case of the BBC and the Scandinavian psb channels) through tightly-controlled delivery formats (as on the first German psb channel ARD with its strictly delimited 'advertising window') to channels where extremely frequent American-style commercial breaks are the norm. Perhaps the most consistent exponent of this last pattern was the German commercial channel RTL where the following combination of soap and adverts was not unusual: adverts / opening credits / adverts / narrative / adverts / narrative / adverts / closing credits / adverts, though not dissimilar patterns can also be found on RTL channels elsewhere. In the course of analysing the fifty or so soaps covered in the previous study, it goes without saying that I simultaneously found myself watching quite literally thousands of adverts. The financial importance of these commercials cannot be underestimated. The advertising revenue produced by the German soap opera *Gute Zeiten, Schlechte Zeiten* and the immediately preceding daily current affairs programme *Explosiv*, for example, is greater than that generated by all of RTL's other programmes taken together.

The theoretical and analytical framework of my earlier project was broadly speaking neo-Gramscian. In other words, it set out from the premise elaborated by early twentieth-century Italian socialist Antonio Gramsci that culture, far from being simply a space of entertainment or 'escapism', is a site (indeed *the* site) where power is most consistently negotiated in contemporary societies. This ongoing negotiation relates in particular to the values competing for leadership – or, to use Gramsci's own terminology, 'hegemony' (Forgacs, 1988) – in the public sphere, a vital element of which is now popular culture with its truly mass contemporary audiences. Though space prevents me from rehearsing at length the theoretical focus or the main findings of that study here, there follows below a brief summary of those conclusions which are of specific relevance to this study of advertising on European television.

My starting point is that we are living in an era of intense hegemonic struggle between an older set of social-democratic practices and discourses which, although clearly dethroned from official politics throughout Western Europe, are by no means utterly defeated, and a new neo-liberal ideology which, although manifestly triumphant in official politics, is encountering stubborn resistance at the level of popular culture where its various claims to hegemony are being vigorously contested. In very general terms, while the old social-democratic hegemony acknowledged the existence of social classes and encouraged – at least at the level of its discourses, if rather less perfectly at the level of its practices – cooperation and solidarity as the central social organising principle, the new neo-liberal hegemony views class as a thing of the past, celebrates individualism, entrepreneurship and 'choice', and directly challenges the view that any part or section of society should support or in any way subsidise any other.

This ideological conflict arises from the emergence of what is sometimes referred to as 'late capitalism' or 'the third stage of capitalism' (Jameson, 1991, following Mandel, 1975), in other words the move from old-style nation-based economic imperialism (the 'second stage of capitalism') to new forms of hypermobile globalising capitalism which simply ignore national boundaries and move at great speed – and no matter what the cost to local populations – to wherever the prospects of maximising returns appears to be greatest. What I would wish to add to recent and current theorisations is the suggestion – easily verifiable, though relatively little appears to have been made of it – that the emergence of late capitalism has caused a profound and almost certainly irreversible split in the old national bourgeoisies: a split between those whose economic – and therefore political, social and cultural – interests continue to be bound by the frontiers of the nation state, and those whose interests – economic, political, social and cultural – now effectively transcend those boundaries. This split can be seen in – among other things – the fissures now appearing within, or the widening gaps opening up between, a number of Western European conservative parties (the traditional parties of the national bourgeoisies). The space created by this puncturing of the Right has, in certain cases, allowed former left-wing parties, under cover of an increasingly brittle patina of rarified social-democratic rhetoric, to align themselves more and more with the globalising fractions of their ruling class. The contradictions arising from these new alignments are at present far from being resolved.

While there can be no simple or direct causal relationship between economic change and cultural output – the result of a mechanical application of the old base-superstructure model which Gramsci himself challenged as a form of 'vulgar Marxism' – it is equally clear that major changes in the economic structures of a society will eventually lead to the appearance of new cultural products through which the new dispensation will attempt to introduce its values and principles into the public sphere. These changes will be subject to slippages and time-lapses of all kinds, always mediated in complex ways and influenced in varying degrees by the co-existence of the old with the new, and the resulting products will enter into competition with those of the former arrangement which is now under attack (we need only think of the wide and varied cultural output which accompanied the rise and eventual consolidation of the industrial bourgeoisies at the beginning of the nineteenth century throughout Western Europe). The success of the new products and their associated values will depend not only on the resources available to those who are either directly or indirectly promoting them — not simply financial or material resources, but also their ability to gain allies in all kinds of gate-keeping positions at all levels of society – but on the resistance, organised or not, of 'cultural consumers' and on their willingness or otherwise to abandon the old products and the values which they in one way or another represent or narrativise.

It is to some extent inevitable that an economic order which transcends the nation state will produce a culture – not *the* culture of a given society, but one of the cultures operating within it – which will attempt to present the governing principles of the nation state as exhausted and irrelevant. Thus while, on an economic level, neo-liberalism (the preferred political form of late capitalism) has led to an increasing unwillingness among firms to finance the welfare arrangements of individual nation states (why should they fund the health care of the local population when within a year or two they may have moved their operations elsewhere?), postmodernism (to use Jameson's term, the *cultural* logic of late capitalism) is likewise characterised by a wide-ranging disengagement from many of the structural features of those states: their histories, their class structures, their literature and art, their definitions of self, even powerful material-symbolic configurations such as their monarchies.

Modernism and Postmodernism

The struggle – and it is indeed a *struggle* – to define both postmodernism and (retrospectively) modernism has provided one of the most intense and complex academic debates of recent years. Positions vary from claiming that there is no such thing as postmodernism, or that it has been invented by academics to keep themselves busy and in jobs or, much more intriguingly, that the academic debate is the expression of a crisis of legitimation among academics themselves in terms of their relationship with the societies within which they are located (Bauman, 1985), to confident announcements that the modern (a code word in this particular debate for national bourgeois capitalism and its political and cultural expressions) and all that went with it (industry, ideology, patriarchy, class struggle, representation, even reality!) have disappeared as we confidently enter an entirely new post-industrial, post-ideological, post-feminist, post-representational age of affluent cosmopolitan consumers enjoying playful relationships with the images and texts which now saturate every moment of their waking lives. Space again does not allow a full discussion of the many and varied ramifications of this debate, but what follows below is a brief summary of what are generally seen as some of the most salient features of postmodern culture which are particularly relevant for the present study. Readers wishing to follow this debate in greater detail can do so in the works of Jameson (1991), Featherstone (1991, 1995), McRobbie (1994), or the many key articles brought together in Featherstone (1988), among a truly vast array of other titles dedicated to this topic.

The Loss of Historicity

Jameson begins the Introduction to his collected theorisings of the postmodern with the contention that, 'It is safest to grasp the concept of the postmodern as an attempt to think the present historically in an age which has forgotten how to think historically in the first place' (1991: ix). Indeed, postmodern culture is characterised most strikingly by a loss of the sense of history either as a process of progress and advancement (the Enlightenment view) or struggle (the Marxist perspective). History appears to have stopped: we are witnessing the 'end of history', not just in the sense that — as Fukujama would claim – liberal democracy has apparently triumphed universally and no further advance is possible, but because there never was any history in the first place anyway. There were only a series of narratives which fooled 'modern' readers into believing that something called history was actually in progress, whereas we now know that they were just narratives after all. Indeed, following Lyotard (1984), the collapse of grand narratives is now often seen as one of the primary features of the postmodern.

What was once seen as history has now become a treasure-trove of styles and fashions: what people were wearing in the nineteenth or early twentieth century, or the kind of furniture they had, for example, is much more important than any social structures emerging from the class struggle at the time (as the flood of period drama on British television recently amply illustrates). Our relationship with the past is now dominated not by analysis or effort towards understanding, but by nostalgia and pastiche. Our sense of time has been replaced by a sense of space, and of flattened-out space at that. The postmodern is the culture of the surface.

The Decentered Self

From the vantage point of the postmodern, the obsession with individual fully coherent identity characteristic of much earlier cultural output is seen as part of a fruitless bourgeois quest for the self as the subject of history. This pointless search – if history is over there is no need for a subject of history – with all its inhibiting consequences has now been overcome, with the result that postmodern culture is characterised by the disappearance of the bounded self. With the new cult of sensation and the emergence of a correspondingly new 'sensorium' (sometimes described as the 'aestheticisation of everyday life') more than one identity – indeed, a limitless number of possible identities which can be donned and doffed at will – are needed to participate fully in the exhilaration of the ever-changing moment. Postmodern culture is therefore characterised by schizo- or even multiphrenic relationships with identity, the refusal to be tied down to a single self, the constant search for ever new identities and their corresponding experiences and sensations. It goes without saying that the decentered self is a godsend to producers and advertisers, since each identity will require its own clothes, its own glasses, its own hairstyle, perhaps even its own differently coloured contact lenses.

The Collapse of the Boundaries between High and Low Art

If the search for the bounded self was part of that tiresome old national-bourgeois culture, even more linked to that socio-cultural formation was the use of art – in particular high art – as a signans of social stratification. In the new postmodern dispensation the old-fashioned discriminatory function of art as so comprehensively theorised by Pierre Bourdieu (1984) is irredeemably *passé*, indeed, every bit as *passé* as class itself, patriarchy, the welfare state, or any other aspect of the boring baggage of a bygone age. Postmodern cultural production is, as a result, characterised by a self-conscious mixing of styles thereby signalling the end of the old hierarchies, by playful quoting and appropriation in its relentless deconstruction of bourgeois sacralities, by the fabrication of texts using other texts in a widespread self-celebratory intertextuality as the gleefully mimetic is preferred to the now entirely suspect creative.

The Death of Representation

If bourgeois culture, in particular literary and cinematic culture, has long been characterised by the search for realism, representation in postmodern culture has become a dead letter and has been confined to the dustbin of non-history. Since there is no objective reality to represent, cultural production now requires the complicitous waiver of reflexivity, where the self-conscious presence of the author is *de rigueur*. In terms of visual narrative there is the emergence of what have been designated 'hyperrealism' or 'hypersignification' (Goldman and Papson, 1994): the use of techniques foregrounding the presence of the camera and indeed of the technicians and directors behind the camera as producers move to a new relationship of playful complicity with their now media-savvy audience.

Soap Operas and Their Adverts

Many adverts currently screening on European television stations easily qualify as postmodern according to one or indeed several of the characteristics outlined above. Many of these adverts are in fact American in origin. While this can on occasions be obvious when they are screened in Continental Europe, it is often masked in the UK by the fact that they are frequently revoiced for the UK audience (indeed, in Scotland they are revoiced using Scottish voices). American adverts – 'small narratives' *par excellence* – are among the most pervasive forms of expression of postmodern culture. The televised version of the 1999 Super Bowl – itself a deeply postmodern experience – featured many such commercials. Thus an advert for millennium-bug-proof Macintosh computers featured a replay of Hal from *2001: A Space Odyssey* recounting sadly how 'global economic disruption' had been caused at the beginning of the new millennium because not everyone was using a Mac. Another striking example was provided by an instalment in the Budweiser ads serial featuring the now long-running battle between the frogs and the lizards: here one lizard's astonishment at the fact that the frogs can speak is dismissed by the largest frog with the information that their previous croaking had been because 'we were reading the script – you should try it some day', while another lizard asks at the end of the ad, 'Now how is that supposed to sell beer?' The Hidden Persuaders of yore have become the wink-wink nudge-nudge buddies of today, congratulating their audience on its ability to see through their advertising strategies.

But a number of adverts of clear European origin can also be seen to display postmodern characteristics. The following is a brief account of a small number of adverts sharing elements of the postmodern which I encountered in the breaks occurring either around or within European soap operas.

As an example of the loss of historicity, an ad for the Fiat Punto on Italy's Canale 5 featured knights riding around on horseback in pursuit of a car, only to find themselves unable to bring their pursuit to a successful conclusion when they have to stop at red traffic lights (much to their queen's scornful disgust). Here we see a playful relationship with history – itself mediated through mediaeval fantasy – clearly in play, with historical barriers removed and jumbled for the delight of the audience and the improvement of Fiat's sales figures. A Finnish ad for margarine, on the other hand, shown on the commercial channel MTV3, features shots of a traditional French farmstead in the rain, complete with rustic furniture and an old-fashioned two-tier coffee-maker inside and box of cabbages outside, accompanied by Jacques Brel singing Prévert's haunting poem *Barbara*. The treasure trove of history is plundered for old-style French chic to sell margarine. Needless to say, none of the deeper issues raised by Prévert's poem itself – for example the ravages of the Second World War in Brest – are explored in any way.

The decentered self is a particularly common advertising theme. Thus a recent ad in the UK featured a train drawing up in an underground station. As the doors open a large number of young women emerge, all wearing different clothes, different glasses, different hairstyles. As they approach the camera it becomes clear that they are all in fact the same young woman wearing a wide range of different outfits. The name of the retail outlet (C&A) then appears on the screen accompanied by the question 'Who do you want to be today?'. A Swedish ad for Spirit deodorant likewise features a young woman setting off for work wearing jeans and a T-shirt. As she leaps through a large hoop carried by some workmen blocking her way on the pavement she transforms into an athlete, suitably kitted out, leaping over a hurdle in a race. We next see her as the couldn't-care-less young thing changing from her casual clothes into a wedding outfit in a taxi, much to the amazement of the older male driver. She ends up arriving in church just in time to get married as the coy-looking bride.

A German ad for Eurocard likewise features a young woman putting on a pink bride's dress for a wedding, only for her dog to come in and place his muddy paws on her bosom. Cut to the shop where, aided by a female friend, she tries on one dress after another, each one more vampish than the one before. She eventually appears before the astonished groom looking like the *femme fatale* from a film noir, at which point the dog makes a reappearance this time to muddy the groom's outfit. It is worthwhile making the point that, although this is indeed a common enough theme in adverts, the only examples encountered to date have attributed the decentered self to women. Indeed, the representation of women would appear to be one of *the* great cultural (and therefore political) battlegrounds of our time.

Many examples of the blurring of the boundaries between high art and low art can also be found. An advert for Sanex skin cream shown on RTL4 in the Netherlands begins with the camera closing in on a classic Italian frieze showing a woman bathing. The paint has become cracked over time, but as the camera moves in to an extreme close up the woman in the painting becomes a real woman soothing her skin with the aforementioned cream. An ad for the Braun iron shown on VT4 in Belgium shows the item in question steaming its way through a Magritte-like landscape of apples and windows, smoothing everything in its path. Quoting is also very commonplace. Thus a recent British ad for the Vauxhall Vectra took the form of a compressed film noir (and was also shot in black and white), while an ad shown on Spanish television for Kas soft drinks was clearly derived from a dragons and dungeons computer game.

In terms of the foregrounding of production, an ad for the ecologically-friendly Renault Mégane shown in the UK featured the car shown against a cartoon background of flowers and bunnies. At the end the cartoon background disappeared and the camera drew back to reveal the studio and another camera apparently shooting the whole thing. A recent Swedish advert for pasta shown on Kanal 4 was shot with the 'restless camera' technique characteristic of productions such as *Hill Street Blues* and *NYPD Blue*, and contained the kind of elliptical and barely understandable conversation sometimes found in *cinéma vérité*.

However, despite the presence of adverts such as those described above, perhaps the most striking finding of this particular piece of research is that, whatever their frequency might be in other parts of the programming schedule, commercials hailing the viewer from within a recognisably postmodern sensibility are extremely *infrequent* in the advertising spaces around or during European soaps. The overwhelming majority of the adverts screened during these slots address a primarily female audience, and they address the 'modern' rather than the 'postmodern' woman, in other words, the woman who is still caught within the dominant paradigms of traditional capitalist society, struggling with all the unfinished business of the nation state. In fact, from this point of view the ads are much *less* progressive than most of the soaps themselves, being deeply embedded in the kind of patriarchal values which the soaps (however imperfectly) often challenge. The bulk of these ads are for household products of all kinds (including foodstuffs) and construct a woman who has to look after the children (nappies), keep the home clean (bleaches), make the meals (bread, butter, cereals, frozen foods), wash the clothes and the dishes (detergents, washing-up liquids), *and* is still required to be elegant, alluring, fragrant and above all have lustrous hair (adverts for shampoos are among those screened with the greatest frequency: indeed, we appear to be living in an era in which women's hair has been fetishised to an unprecedented degree).

Conclusions

A number of conclusions can be drawn from this short study. A first, admittedly somewhat subsidiary but nonetheless rather surprising finding, is that soap operas' male viewers are being largely ignored by the advertisers. Figures from around Europe show that, as a general rule, around 30% of soap opera viewers are male. Their symbolic annihilation from the adverts is virtually complete. Secondly, recognisably postmodern adverts are much less in evidence in the slots around soap operas than they are in the television schedule as a whole and, thirdly, to the extent that they are present at all they are noticeably more common in the television channels of northern Europe than in those of the Mediterranean. How are these differences to be accounted for?

The answer lies, to some extent, in the audience profile of the soaps – or more precisely in how this is perceived by the advertisers – and to a greater extent in the soaps' broader relationship with the popular culture, and via that with the political culture of the countries in which they are shown. A review of the items advertised in, and an analysis of the dominant mode of address of, ads operating within a postmodern sensibility would show that the bulk (though not necessarily all) address a relatively young and relatively affluent audience, and soap operas also addressing such an audience such as the German soap *Gute Zeiten, Schlechte Zeiten* – itself a postmodern soap (O'Donnell, 1999: 56–64) – attract many more adverts of this kind than others. But European soaps in general attract a much more varied audience, one which is predominantly adult and demographically complex, and for whom the endlessly recurring narrativisation of the problems of 'modern' societies still constitutes a powerful pole of attraction. History is by no means over in soaps, or for their audiences. Indeed, the narratives of the soaps themselves are dominated by different elements of the unfinished business of the nation states, all the unresolved (and indeed unresolvable) problems generated by the unbridgeable gap between the discourses of bourgeois capitalist democracy and the practices (institutions, policies) which this socio-economic formation itself allows.

Soaps are, for example, frequently mired in the problems of patriarchal relations of authority, a standpoint from where the postmodern post-feminist women deciding 'who they want to be today' appear rather like creatures from another planet. This is a very hostile environment for postmodern ads, indeed for the postmodern in general. While adverts can in no sense be said to mirror reality, they are, as Giaccardi rightly argues, 'discourses upon reality' (1995: 127), and the discourses of modern soaps and postmodern adverts resist compagination. And since – despite the recent incursion of Spanish banks into the economies of a number of South American countries – the presence of transnational capital is much less in evidence in Mediterranean societies than in those of the north of Europe, it would be logical to assume, if the present analysis is correct, that there would be even less space for the postmodern in those societies as a result. As soap opera characters and viewers struggle endlessly with the contradictions of the modern condition, the postmodern celebration of its new liberated sensorium sits uneasily with this engagement with the real problems of real people's ongoing lives. And while we can be sure that many soap viewers who tape their favourite programme when they are out will fast-forward through the ads on their return, there is little or no chance of them ever fast-forwarding through the soap itself.

The view of the postmodern offered here is a predominantly negative one, and corresponds closely with my own view of neo-liberalism and its abusive and predatory economic practices. However, transnational capitalism is not a reversible phenomenon: it is here to stay, and there can be little doubt that, like both the first and the second phases of capitalism before it, it is dramatically increasing the productive capacity of those societies in which it is installed, albeit at the expense of those on whom – both internally and externally – it preys. It is important not to take too one-sided a view. The postmodern – like any other cultural phenomenon – is a site of contestation, and the breaking down of many of the old barriers and the old truths – what Jameson refers to as the 'relief of the postmodern' (1991: 313) – has been experienced by many – particularly those remote from either the political or the geographical 'centre' and its particular set of 'truths' – as at least potentially liberatory. There is indeed, as Betz argues, a 'postmodernism of resistance' (1992: 109–10). It seems to me to be perfectly legitimate – varying slightly on Zygmunt Bauman's theme – to see the theoretical struggle to define the modern and the postmodern as an *academic* manifestation of the debate on where late capitalism is taking us in relation to the values and structures of still existing nation states. But it is crucial in my view not to allow the debate to be defined by the competing world-views of different fractions of the national bourgeoisies. This is not a two-cornered fight. The third contestant is represented by the viewers of both soaps and ads alike: the working classes of Western Europe and beyond. It is neither a question of celebrating the end of the nation state, nor of wondering how its unfinished business can be resolved using the resources of the past, but of achieving sufficient control of the new resources released by late capitalism so that they are used for the improvement of the lives of the many rather than the few.

References

Bauman, Z., 'Is there a Postmodern Sociology?', *Theory, Culture and Society*, 5:2 & 3 (1985).

Betz, G-B., 'Postmodernism and the New Middle Classes', *Theory, Culture and Society*, 9:2 (1992).

Bourdieu, P., *Distinction: a Social Critique of the Judgement of Taste*, London: Routledge & Kegan Paul, 1984.

Featherstone, M. (ed.), *Postmodernism*, London: Sage, 1988.

Featherstone, M., *Consumer Culture and Postmodernism*, London, Sage, 1991.

Featherstone, M., *Undoing Culture: Globalization, Postmodernism and Identity*, London: Sage, 1995.

Forgacs, D., *A Gramsci Reader: Selected Writings 1916–1935*, London: Lawrence & Wishart, 1988.

Giaccardi, C., 'Television Advertising and the Representation of Social Reality: A Comparative Study' in *Theory, Culture and Society*, 12:1 (1995).

Goldman, R. & Papson, S., 'Advertising in the Age of Hypersignification' in *Theory, Culture and Society*, 11:3 (1994).

Jameson, F., *Postmodernism, or the Cultural Logic of Late Capitalism*, London: Verso Duke University Press, 1991.

Lyotard, J-F., *The Postmodern Condition: a Report on Knowledge*, Manchester: Manchester University Press, 1984.

McRobbie, A., *Postmodernism and Popular Culture*, London: Routledge, 1994.

Mandel, E., *Late Capitalism*, London: Verso, 1975.

O'Donnell, H., *Good Times, Bad Times: Soap Operas and Society in Western Europe*, London: Leicester University Press, 1999.

14 Fools, Philosophers and Fanatics
Modes of Masculinity in World Cup-Related Advertising

Anne M. White
University of Bradford

'All that I know about morality and the obligations of man, I know from football'

Albert Camus

Writing in general terms about the commercial opportunities afforded by the World Cup, Meg Carter (1998) of *The Independent* had humorously predicted that the 1998 sporting event would effectively amount to 'A month of advertising with some great soccer thrown in'. As the tournament neared its climax, the results of a UK survey published in *Marketing Week*[1] suggested that many of those interviewed would have considered her words an accurate reflection of their personal perception of the situation. Some 66% of those questioned thought that 'too many manufacturers [were] jumping on the bandwagon' and half of the sample interviewed agreed that they would be 'glad when it was all over': the football fever which had broken out in June had evidently developed by mid-July into a serious case of 'football fatigue' (Millar, 1998). This reaction was not surprising given that those watching the World Cup coverage on ITV had been exposed to dozens of commercials shown before and after the matches and during half-time in which football had been used to sell everything from Coca-Cola to cars. Perhaps this was only to be expected given that these breaks had been pitched to advertisers as primetime slots for those wishing to market products intended to appeal to what was assumed to be a predominantly male audience. More specifically, they were sold as a means of presenting advertisers with a golden opportunity to target that most elusive group of consumers: young men with disposable incomes who normally watch a relatively small amount of television. The rarity of this audience profile was reflected in the prices commanded by these premium slots, with, for example, a 30-second spot during the England versus Romania game costing £180,000 as opposed to the customary £85,000 for a comparable break in standard programming (Martin, 1998).

It should be noted, however, that there was some debate in the British press prior to and during the tournament concerning the validity of the assumptions being made about the demographics of the audience, a debate which was fuelled in part at least by the results of a survey carried out by the advertising agency, J. Walter Thompson, in which 40% of the women interviewed said that they intended to watch all the World Cup matches while 62% said that they wanted to view at least some of them, figures which suggest that female interest in the event was much stronger than had been anticipated (Martin, 1998). Nonetheless, even a cursory analysis of the sample of British television adverts, broadcast in these pre- and post-match slots or during half-time while the tournament was on, strongly suggests that advertisers believed they had a captive young male audience and had set out to target this group. Beer, fast food and snacks feature prominently in these commercial breaks as do sports-related items (football boots, Isotonic Lucozade) together with 'boy toys' such as cars and computer hardware/software. Moreover, almost half of the spots in the sample could be said to contain one or more elements which could be interpreted as a direct or indirect reference to the world of football. This is without including the Vauxhall break-bumpers (ads shown at the beginning and end of each commercial break), all of which used football-related elements.

Fowles (1996: xiv) has suggested that 'the future may know us through our advertising and popular culture' and in this article, I intend to focus mainly on this particular sample of UK television spots with their links to the world of football in order to examine what, if anything, they might have to say about how different modes of masculinity are constructed at the intersection of sport and advertising and represented televisually at the end of the twentieth century. A sample of French television spots was recorded at the same time, from TF1 via satellite, and where these are thought to provide a particularly interesting comparison, reference will be made to them. However, for a number of reasons, a truly comparative analysis is somewhat problematic.

Firstly, there is the crucial difference regarding the importance of the role which football as a sport has played within the culture of France and the United Kingdom as a whole, to say nothing of the distinctive football. One English journalist noted that with few exceptions, 'Football in France is a pastime, not a passion' (Moore, 1998) and the French sociologist, Patrick Mignon, agreed that for his fellow citizens, due partly at least to reasons of history, 'Football is just one of a number of sports' and does not generally provoke the intensity of emotional response associated with the game in England in particular (cited in Moore, 1998).

For advertisers, then, these pre-, post- and mid-match slots in France did not have the same potential for capturing a young masculine audience, a fact which is reflected in the much less-narrowly targeted advertising in the sample. Certainly there were some male-orientated spots for sportswear, cars and computer hardware/software together with a small number of commercials for men's toiletries, including after-shave, shaving foam and deodorant, a category which did not feature in the UK sample at all. However, specifically football-related advertising appeared much less frequently on TF1 than on ITV. In the UK sample of spots analysed, there was ample evidence of the attempts being made by advertisers to suggest a link, however tenuous, between the product being promoted and the World Cup. Most companies advertising on TF1 seem to have adopted what might be termed the All-or-Nothing strategy, i.e. they either became Official World Cup Sponsors and fully exploited this link in their commercials or opted for campaigns which avoided any references to football.

A relatively few companies advertised in both countries. It is particularly interesting to contrast how the multinational McDonalds, one of the twelve Official World Cup sponsors, used the corresponding slots in France and the UK to promote its products to what it perceived to be very different groups of potential consumers. The company's UK television campaign was clearly aimed at those who are fans of both football and fast food, since their spot featured the Captain of the England squad, Alan Shearer, waxing lyrical about the unique qualities of the company's best known product, the Big Mac.

In the French commercial, however, the only reference to football takes the form of the France '98 logo which is seen together with the caption *Restaurant Officiel de la Coupe du Monde* in the closing caption shot and the target audience in this case would appear to be those who would not usually consider eating fast food. The emphasis throughout seems to be on convincing French viewers that McDonalds has more to offer than just hamburgers. The McDonald's example clearly indicates that advertisers in the two countries believed they were attempting to target very different types of viewers, although the timing of the commercial breaks was similar. Other products that featured in both UK and French samples were the chocolate bar, Snickers, and L'Oréal hair shampoo, both of which will be referred to later.

A second complication arises when attempting a comparative analysis between the ITV and TF1 spots, one which results not from socio-historical but from more recent developments in French advertising legislation. The advertising of alcohol is not allowed on French terrestrial television channels and the *Loi Evin*, which came into force in France in January 1993, also forbids any advertising of alcoholic drinks in sports' stadia or in connection with sporting events. The TF1 sample therefore contained no spots for alcohol, whereas adverts for beer made up a substantial and significant proportion of the ITV slots.

Moreover, because the vast majority of beer ad spots made overt references to the world of football, they proved to be a particularly interesting source of material for analysing the way in which masculinity is constructed televisually in this textual interface between popular culture and consumer culture, but one which had no counterpart in the world of French advertising. This article will mainly be concerned with an analysis of the sample of ITV television spots, examples of how they were received and with an examination of the various modes of masculinity represented therein. These different modes can, I believe, be aptly characterised as fools, philosophers and fanatics and it is to the first of these that we now turn our attention.

Fools

In the sample two of those who appear to fall into the category of fool as 'a person who is made to appear ridiculous' are, in fact, famous footballers. Interestingly in both instances, although the individual in question is given the chance to display his footballing abilities, these are presented in unconventional contexts that bring a humorous dimension to the commercial. At the same time, though, these situations also draw on particular stereotypical notions of masculinity as they are commonly represented in media texts and popular discourse about football. Thus the advert for Isotonic Lucozade (one of a number of so-called 'sports' drinks claiming to re-energise those engaged in physical activity and targeted at young, though not necessarily male, consumers) casts Alan Shearer, who is from the North East, as the latest in a long line of footballing legends from the North. His own grim determination has apparently been shaped by an environment in which everything from the overcast sky to the bleak urban landscape is also unremittingly grim. Framed by a backdrop of terraced houses, this working-class lad has no time for new-fangled training methods, so he hones his skills by repeatedly kicking a football at a rug in order to beat out the dust, urged on by an older man who bellows 'Welly it, man!' in a Geordie accent. In accordance with Adams, we find the accumulation of clichés pertaining to Northernness presented in the advert signalling to viewers that this is comic exaggeration (Adams, 1985). It is common knowledge that the archetypal amateur player he portrays here disappeared long ago from the world of football, if indeed he ever really existed outside of the realms of popular myth. In this advert, then, Shearer evokes a mode of masculinity which can no longer form part of the repertoire of roles open to today's football player, who has been transformed into a valuable commodity in an international market. Along with the element of ridicule here, then, we can perhaps also detect a certain nostalgia for 'The Good Old Days' when local footballers played for love not money and relied on natural ability rather than high-performance footwear. The slogan chosen for the product, 'Dedicated to sport', could also be said to articulate these two notions simultaneously. On one level, it conveys the fact that in this commercial Shearer is only 'playing the fool' since fans know that he is really an international footballer who is 'dedicated to sport'. However, on another level, it also suggests perhaps something of that nostalgic subtext, a desire to return to a time when footballers were solely 'dedicated to sport'.

The Nike campaign which ran in both the UK and France for the duration of the World Cup offered up another version of the fool, personified by the Brazilian footballer, Ronaldo, in a series of adverts featuring him and his team mates. Like Shearer, he gets to display his footballing talents but outside of the usual confines of the soccer stadium. He is seen in a beach kickabout, at one stage running with the ball tucked inside his sweatshirt to confuse his fellow players; in another scenario he plays goalkeeper and, much to the amusement of all concerned, proves to be spectacularly inept in this position. In these adverts, there are no attempts made to draw viewers' attention to the stereotypical nature of the portrayal. Indeed, quite the opposite, since the aim here appears to be to present what is effectively a set of clichés as an unproblematic reflection of reality: in other words, we are meant to believe that this is Ronaldo simply 'being himself '.

It is worth noting that at the time these adverts were being televised, the sports' pages of the press were full of articles concerning the enormous amounts of money which Ronaldo was making from his career as the latest sporting icon for Nike. As a result, one might also choose to read these images as yet another example of a footballer choosing merely to 'play the fool', taking part in an elaborate performance in

133

which he imitates and sells back to the advertising and media industries those very stereotypes of masculinity which it itself has helped to create and maintain.

Philosophers

In both the McDonalds and Nike adverts, the footballers in question are presented as doers rather than thinkers. These are men who express themselves through actions not words and the emphasis is on their physical abilities rather than their intellectual qualities. To borrow one of Nike's own slogans, they 'Just do it'. However, one can identify a second mode of masculinity in the adverts that feature soccer celebrities. This is the category of the player turned philosopher, the footballer who is shown talking about the game rather than playing it. Somewhat in keeping with popular national stereotypes of the English as pragmatists and the French as intellectuals, the tendency seems to be for French rather than English footballers to be characterised seriously in this way as philosophers and holders of social values.

In France, the whole of the Adidas campaign developed specifically for that country (since the sportswear company was the official sponsor of the French national side) was based around scenes featuring monologues by various members of the team, on the subject of football and what winning or losing meant to them. The slogan used in one of the adverts – La victoire est en nous – and the style in which it is written, is reminiscent of the urban graffiti which was seen throughout Kassovitz's hard-hitting 1995 film about contemporary *banlieue* life, *La Haine*. Both Kassovitz's film and the Adidas campaign which chose to emphasise the multi-ethnic composition of France's 'Rainbow Team' had an underlying anti-racist theme. The Adidas adverts seen in the UK, on the other hand, were stylishly shot in black and white and featured high-profile international players in bizarre scenarios evocative of video games or science-fiction films. They generally made little impact on the popular imagination and were derided by one sports' journalist for featuring images of 'macho, futuristic automatons' and a slogan which was 'nonsense' (Parker, 1998). Similarly futuristic scenarios and techniques (e.g. morphing) were also used in the adverts for Puma Celerator football boots and the Ford Ka car.

Another advert featuring a French footballer cast as philosopher which attracted much media attention was the L'Oréal campaign featuring David Ginola. Adverts for the company's hair care range fronted by Ginola were included in the recorded sample for both France and the UK but the images and words used in each case were slightly altered as the product being promoted was a different one. In the UK version, the hair shampoo is described as being 'two-in-one' (shampoo and conditioner) and it can hardly be coincidence that it is being endorsed by a celebrity who could himself be described as 'two-in-one': a football player-cum-media star. Indeed, the commercial makes a feature of Ginola's ambiguous status opening with a shot of the man himself proclaiming directly to camera: 'I'm a footballer not a movie star' as he stands centre stage in an enormous football stadium. However, his statement is blatantly contradicted by the fact that he is not wearing a football kit but is carefully coiffeured and dressed in a designer-suit. The opening scene then cuts immediately to shots of him in dark glasses in the glare of paparazzi flashbulbs. Elsewhere in the advert, the nearest Ginola is seen to get to sporting action is during a game of table football in a chic café.

Dave Hill's article makes particularly interesting reading in the context of the present discussion on advertising and modes of masculinity. With reference to Ginola's mixed reputation as a footballer, he writes: 'His critics regard him as a luxury item, big on style but short on substance and reluctant to put in the hard graft which our domestic football culture has traditionally prized' (Hill, 1998). His comments here seem to reflect a nostalgia for a more authentic and masculine version of the sport which is not 'short on substance' but based on 'hard graft', a 'traditionally prized' quality.

Referring elsewhere in the article to Ginola's reputation for 'diving' or deliberately and theatrically falling when tackled, he comments that: 'his writhings when felled frequently resemble those of the "dying swan" scene in that well-known ballet.' In this image, Ginola is transposed from a realm popularly constructed as masculine (football) to one perceived to be feminine (ballet) and other descriptions of him in the same article as 'extremely pretty' or a 'prima donna' function in a similar way to feminise the footballer and to place a question mark over his masculinity. Even the title of the article 'I've got to stay in to wash my hair' evokes clichéd 'girl talk', signalling Hill's implied argument that footballers who wish to be taken seriously as footballers (and as men, perhaps?) should not appear in commercials for shampoo.

Comparing and contrasting these examples of adverts featuring famous football players, and the reactions to them, one might draw a tentative conclusion. There seems to be a grudging acceptance that footballers can be media stars as long as this is not seen to imply too great a shift in the notion of masculinity that has been traditionally ascribed to this role in the realms of popular culture. However, footballers who are media stars must not deliberately give the game away. The pretence that they are ultimately dedicated to sport must be maintained by some means and above all, this dual or ambiguous status should not be flaunted or openly celebrated, as in the L'Oréal campaign. I will return to this point later.

Fanatics

In the adverts to be analysed under the final category, the focus shifts from the footballers to the fans who watch them. It should be said that although there were some isolated examples of representations of female fans being shown in both French and UK commercials, the images seen were predominantly of males. The spectators represented in these adverts can be further subdivided into two distinct categories, Men of Words and Men of Action, a split somewhat similar to the philosopher/fool divide observed previously. In the first group, I would place those representations of what are sometimes disparagingly referred to in the footballing fraternity as the New Fans[2] or *soccerati*. These articulate football supporters appear to have been inspired by, or may have found a voice in, writers like Nick Hornby, author of the best-seller *Fever Pitch*, which became famous for raising the art of football writing to new heights and some would claim for providing a number of telling insights into the state of contemporary masculinity. The Men of Words featured in the Carlsberg Lager UK campaign seemed to be living proof of the suggestion made by one journalist that football was set to become 'the Esperanto of the new millennium, speaking across all boundaries' (Mitchell, 1998) since it shows us that male fans the world over, from Icelandic fishermen mending their nets to African tribesmen hunting on the plains, are shown to have but one topic of conversation: endless speculation about the composition of the England World Cup team. The advert plays in a number of ways with stereotypes of nationality, as have many other recent advertising campaigns for beer, which allow it to be read, it could be argued, either as knowing postmodern irony or unreconstructed naive nationalism. However we choose to interpret it, the advert also hints at something of the reality of the so-called Third Age of Broadcasting, in which the revolution in communications technology means that a sporting occasion like the World Cup is a truly global televisual event.

Probably those who have benefited most from what one writer dismissed as this 'fashion for endless analysis of the new-found intricacies of a game once regarded as uncomplicated, not to say plain dumb' (Leapman, 1998) have been the professional Men of Words, the sports' presenters. It is hardly surprising given their current prominence in sports' broadcasting that these also make an appearance in the adverts, at least in the UK sample. Thus in the British commercial for Snickers a wildly enthusiastic football commentator insists on giving a frame-by-frame account of a particular move, analysing the same shot from a variety of angles, one after another, on his sophisticated viewing equipment while members of the England squad stand in the background, bored and redundant.

Although clearly intended to be a humorous comment on the verbosity of television sports' commentators, the advert also raises an interesting issue regarding the role which football now occupies in the UK. Partly because of the fact that since the 1960s, more people have experienced the game through television and through the media in general rather than through attendance at live matches, Russell has argued that: 'By most criteria the main significance of football in contemporary British society is as a television show' (Russell, 1997). Thus the advert suggests that mediatisation of sport, and of football in particular, has resulted in a bizarre role reversal which means that the football players – the real thing – find themselves relegated to the sidelines while the simulation of the event – the images which they have created – is foregrounded in endless combinations (multiple camera angles, freeze frames, slow motion, close ups) which require expert interpretation by a commentator who is now the star of the show.

The fact that football is now largely a mediatised spectacle for many fans is also reflected in the way in which the relatively small amount of sporting action which does figure in these commercials is represented, imitating as it does the televisual presentation of the sport. As Ian Parker (1998) noted: 'In TV football, the heart of the game is not the action, but the action replayed. In a sport that pays millions for speed, anything of significance happens very, very slowly, and often. Wise advertisers, knowing this, tell splendid emotional stories using replayed, repeated, suspended, decelerated action'. However, it is perhaps significant that in the UK sample, the number of adverts featuring what was happening on the terraces outnumbered those showing the action on the pitch. In many of these 'splendid emotional stories', the fans, formerly considered to be a mere supporting cast, seem to have taken over centre stage from the footballers, and to have become themselves the Men of Action, a situation which seems to be acknowledged by the Coca-Cola campaign which posed the question: 'If there was a World Cup for fans would you qualify?'

Fans have, of course, always played a crucial and active role in sporting events but the mediatisation of football now allows them the possibility to see themselves 'being there' as part of the spectacle and performing. Post-Heysell and Hillsborough, this performance in the 1990s has been characterised by the creation of a carnivalesque mode of fandom in which dressing up plays an important part, whether it be clown-like face paint and garishly coloured wigs or replica kits and designer labels. In the case of the Coca-Cola campaign, this performance also included repeated images of fans in what might be loosely termed national dress, intended to stress the global appeal not only of football but also of their own product. In an advert which blends footage of crowds with shots of individual fans, the focus is on the agony and the ecstasy which the game excites: the spectacle is not provided by the footballing action but by the emotions it arouses. There was also recognition by advertisers in the UK of the fact that for the vast majority, these emotional highs and lows would be experienced from an armchair or in the company of friends at the local bar or pub. So, there were a number of spots that included images which seemed designed to stress that watching football on TV was not necessarily the second-best option or a passive experience but one which had the power to actively engage the emotions of the viewer. The best example of this was the Budweiser commercial with its scenes of spectators in different countries watching a football match being broadcast on television. We don't see any of the action on the pitch nor see the goals being scored – we merely watch and hear the varied reactions of the fans. Like the Coca-Cola spot, the advert attempted to convince us that regardless of race, colour or creed we can all belong to the fraternity of football fanatics or as the slogan-writers succinctly put it: 'One World, One Game, One Beer'.

In World Cup advertising, according to Parker (1998), 'football becomes the thing which it always promises to be in real life, but never is: a euphoric spectacle, whose entertainment is lodged in the event itself, rather than in anticipation of the event, or memories of it'. An idealised experience of masculine football fandom and spectatorship is certainly portrayed as 'The Real Thing' in the Coca-Cola advert, which presents a world in which emotional intensity is not accompanied by displays of physical aggression or violence, and in which the only significant source of difference between men is the team they support. Here again we can perhaps recognise a certain nostalgic handling of the 'community–unity' motif highlighted by the loss of membership of an imagined community of men, the brotherhood of supporters who once filled the terraces. However, the Budweiser spot and a number of similar adverts encourage male viewers to envisage themselves as part of a new virtual community, one which is the product of contemporary transglobal communications and mediatised sport in the televisual age. These adverts, then, are perhaps intended to act as a form of reassurance for male viewers: society, technology, even masculinity itself may be in a state of flux and transition, but the eternal triangle – Beer, Blokes and The Beautiful Game – remains solid.

Conclusion

It can be argued that the sense of nostalgia which underlies some of this World Cup-related advertising reflects some very real contemporary anxieties felt by football fans about the rapidly changing state of play in the game: when we are uncertain about the present, it is all the more comforting to take refuge in an imagined past. However, beyond this, I also believe that these anxieties surrounding the transitional state of this traditionally male-oriented popular cultural form might be said to be indicative of more wide-ranging concerns about the current uncertain state of masculinity itself. This is demonstrated particularly well, I think, by the reaction of male journalists to the David Ginola L'Oréal campaign. By representing him as 'two-in-one' or both/and, the advert disrupts and moreover flaunts the disruption of the neat categorisations or binary oppositions normally demanded by the discourse of this popular cultural domain: you can be *either* a football player *or* a media star but when you are seen to be blurring the distinguishing lines between the two, confusion inevitably results. Although this is never openly acknowledged, the discourse which the male journalists use gives the game away, providing evidence of where their real anxieties might lie, namely that allowing slippage in one domain – that of football – might lead to slippage in another – that of gender, a whole other ball game.

Notes

1   NOP in conjunction with *Marketing Week* interviewed 1,000 people after the England versus Colombia match on 29 June 1998.

2   'New Fan can be seen on television in celebrity garms, spouting second-hand opinions, or in pubs deconstructing tactics in a totally fabulous way, or in table-footie bars in a regressed, cappucino'd-up state'. Emma Lindsey, 'Pity the great old game in a world of New Fan, fat cats and pseuds' *The Observer*, 7 June 1998, p.5.

References

Adams, E., *Television and The North*, Centre for Contemporary Cultural Studies, Media Series Stencilled Occasional Papers 78, February 1985, pp. 2–5 & pp. 32–5.

Carter, M.,'A month of advertising with some great soccer thrown in', *The Independent*, 27 April 1998, pp. 2–3.

Fowles, J., *Advertising and Popular Culture*, Thousand Oaks, London & New Delhi: Sage, 1996.

Hill, D., 'I've got to stay in to wash my hair', *The Observer* , 11 January 1998, p. 12.

Kelner, M., 'Screen Break: Vauxhall drives to distraction', *The Guardian*, 29 June 1998, p. 11.

Leapman, M., 'Who'll win the TV World Cup?', *Independent on Sunday*, 31 May 1998, p. 26.

Martin, M., 'Women and the football pitch', *The Independent*, 30 June 1998, p. 19.

Millar, S., 'Advertisers drain the Cup dry', *The Guardian*, 10 July 1998, p. 3.

Mitchell, K., 'Football is the Esperanto for the new millennium', *The Observer*, 12 July 1998, p. 6.

Moore, G., 'Stage is set for the finest to flourish', *The Independent*, 8 June 1998, p. 10.

Parker, I., 'In a sport that pays millions for speed, anything of significance happens very, very slowly', *The Observer*, 21 June 1998, p. 12.

Russell, D., *Football and the English: A Social History of Association Football in England, 1863–1995*, Preston: Carnegie, 1997.